D0188151

Homemade Joy

— Journey to Happiness —

By
PAUL H. HOLDEMAN
And
JOE LEWANDOWSKI
And
MARK BREIMHORST

First Edition

Published by Canopy Productions
Fort Collins, Colorado

Library of Congress Catalogue–in-Publication Data
Homemade Joy: Creating the Life You Want / Holdeman, Paul –
First Edition
p. cm.
ISBN# 0-9665697-0-9 $11.95

Self-actualization
Holdeman, Paul
Self Help, title

Printed in the United States of America
God Bless

Homemade Joy

Journey to Happiness

By
Paul H. Holdeman, Joe Lewandowski
and Mark Breimhorst

Published By
Canopy Productions
Post Office Box 1261
Fort Collins, Colorado 80522

COVER DESIGN BY DOLORES ROWLAND

TYPOGRAPHY BY GAIL BLINDE

PROOFING BY DEBBIE DIXON-DOBKINS

BACK PAGE PHOTO BY VALERIE FATE-BEERS

PRINTING BY PIONEER IMPRESSIONS

TO ORDER BOOKS

To order more copies of this book, send a check
made out to Canopy Productions for $11.95,
plus $4.00 shipping and handling for the first book
and $2.00 for each additional book.

Mail to:
CANOPY PRODUCTIONS
P.O. BOX 1261
FORT COLLINS, CO 80522

Allow 4-6 weeks for delivery.

SEMINARS

Paul Holdeman and Mark Breimhorst are available for lectures,
seminars and workshops. Contact Canopy Productions for
information and scheduling.

Please feel free to send your comments,
we would love to hear from you!

Canopy Productions
P.O. Box 1261
Fort Collins, Colorado 80522
Email: pandh@frii.com

Contents

FOREWARD

For the past fifteen years or so, people have been asking me to share my "philosophy" of life in the form of a book. Although I enjoy public speaking, I have a hard time putting my thoughts and experiences in writing. I guess I am like those actors who cannot go to any of their own movies. Once I have given a talk, I can never listen to the recording of what I have said. About two years ago, two friends, Joe Lewandowski and Mark Breimhorst approached me and my wife Helen with the idea of writing this book. It has been a labor of love for all of us and we hope you enjoy reading it as much as we have enjoyed writing it!

– Paul Holdeman

ACKNOWLEDGMENTS

The energy that we call "life" flows not only from generation to generation but also from friend to friend and acquaintance to acquaintance. In an attempt to express my deep appreciation for all those to whom I am indebted, I can only choose representatives from various fields of activity. I am especially grateful to my wife Helen for her honest reflections given without criticism. To our children; Bonnie, Tim, Mark and Priscilla for being my laboratory – sometimes consciously and sometimes unconsciously. To Mark Breimhorst for insisting that this book be written and to Joe Lewandowski who did the bulk of the writing after hours and hours of interviewing me. To Lynn Kendall and Pam Timms, my colleagues who joined me in creating a workplace that is fun and for having the integrity to lovingly challenge inconsistencies in my thinking. To teenagers who shared their deepest, honest thoughts and feelings with me. I am also particularly thankful for my parents and older siblings for having the courage to question old ways of thinking and to risk the new, thereby being my models. Finally, to all the people along the way who dared to share their frustrations, struggles and triumphs with me, I thank you.

– Paul Holdeman

INTRODUCTION

Be bold and mighty forces will come to your aid.
UNKNOWN

In 1950, two years after we were married, my wife
Helen and I volunteered for a service opportunity presented
by our church. We were placed in a rural area outside
Gulfport, Mississippi. Our job was to recognize the worth
of each individual, be they black or white. We were also to
help work out the adjustments that would be required
should the United States Supreme Court strike down the
concept of "separate but equal" in regard to race relations.

The camp where we were sent included a workshop, a
dormitory and some cabins. We managed the camp and
organized the work of volunteers. Many of the people we
worked with lived in poverty. Many houses had no electric-
ity, no toilets, no window screens and some had no doors.
The local school for blacks was a cinder block building.
There were no chalkboards, no toilets and more students
than desks. We installed outdoor toilets, a lunchroom,
makeshift chalkboards and built chairs to compensate for
the lack of desks. Throughout the county we worked with
dozens of families to install sanitary facilities in their homes
in an attempt to control a parasite known as hookworm.

The work fit my idea of service, and it was work that we loved. We felt what we were doing was significant. With our service, we expressed our spirit and we shared our love. Our job was not to be missionaries. We worked. We provided service. We had fun. We laughed a lot. "Being of service" made an enormous amount of sense to us. We didn't ask for anything. We only sought to serve and to learn.

In the small community in that area we had become well known and I would occasionally speak to a local congregation. About a year after we arrived, church leaders approached me to become an assistant to the aging minister. As was the custom, a vote was taken. The congregation, about 65 people, voted unanimously to call me as their assistant minister. I was 27 years old, and becoming a minister was not what I wanted to do – even though I believed in providing service within the church. But how could I say no to 65 people? I had been taught to believe in "corporate wisdom." Certainly, I thought, if 65 people voted unanimously for me, then it must be God's will. I had been taught not to trust my own desires. I should have felt very flattered and praised, but the vote brought me little joy. It took me six weeks to decide. Finally, with great reluctance, I accepted. Despite my misgivings, I threw myself wholeheartedly into the work. I delivered sermons that I considered upbeat, trying to deliver an optimistic message, but I didn't believe in my heart that what I was saying worked. I quoted liberally from the Bible, but my words rang hollow.

Wherever I went, I thought I should be "witnessing." On the street, or in the doctor's office I would hand out cards with inscriptions of Bible passages. To perfect strangers I would say, "Have you been saved by our Lord,

Jesus Christ?" I knew what I was preaching was not true to my experience. It felt dishonest, and it was far from a joyful experience. That provided a great paradox for me. The Bible stated that doing God's work was supposed to be a joyful experience, but I felt nothing of the sort. At the camp, the work – the service – was fun. As a minister I was miserable. I was doing what I thought I was supposed to be doing. I believed I was following God's calling and the calling of the church. I was doing what other people told me I should be doing, what other people told me I was good at. I was doing what was expected of me. And I was miserable.

My actions and my feelings reflected what I had been taught. I had been taught that humans are prone to evil, and if given the chance, would lead evil lives. We were not to think about ourselves, about our desires, or about what would make us happy. It was our duty to witness, to tell people to commit their lives to God and be saved. We also were taught to be of service to others.

I asked myself: Wasn't this service? Wasn't this the same as fixing houses and schools in the countryside? Hadn't I been "called" to do God's work on earth? If someone didn't preach to the people, who would?

The harder I tried to be a minister, the less satisfaction I found. So I fell back on what I'd learned in my early training and used this Bible verse as an excuse: "God works in mysterious ways his wonders to perform." I believed that because I was doing the "Lord's work" the devil was going to give me a rough time, and consequently, struggle was inevitable in my life.

The church I served didn't believe in paying its ministers. To accept pay would be to "commercialize the gospel."

To support my family, I bought into one of those network marketing plans to sell food supplements. I wasn't cut out for this either. I proceeded to lose money for 36 months in a row. Over the next few years I borrowed $10,000, which was a good sum then. With two children, my obligation to the church, and a big debt, I was in severe stress. None of this looked like the road to salvation. I was immobilized with failure. Each day I was consumed with thoughts of living my life out as a failure. Everywhere I turned I found the evidence – debt, unhappiness, doubt. I was spending other people's money, and I wasn't paying it back. On Sundays I continued to preach "the biblical truth." And every day I became increasingly aware that it didn't work for me. I felt no joy in this supposed path to glory. For three years, Helen supported me in my struggles, but at some level, perhaps unconsciously, she knew that her support was enabling me to remain in my paralyzed state. In the summer of 1954, Helen went to visit her parents in Denver. While there she found job opportunities that would help pull us out of our financial mess. She decided not to return to Mississippi. Helen didn't want a divorce; her intent was to follow her own path and do what was best for our family. She knew that the support she had been providing me was no longer helpful. After two weeks alone in Mississippi, my rage finally burst. "God damn it, God, where are you?" I screamed as I drove down the road between Gulfport and Biloxi. No response was forthcoming. Now guilt for having addressed Almighty God in such a profane manner added to the pain and disappointment of the moment. This is where I had come to after just three years of trying to be what I didn't want to be. Nothing made sense to me. Frustration, depression, anger, and fear engulfed me. I finally came to the realization that I couldn't go on in that state. Then I started talking: "Well God, I guess we're partners, but it sure doesn't feel like I've got one. You don't take my hand when I reach out to you, you don't answer when I pray to you. Why should I think I've got a partner?" I thought on that for awhile. It was a question I'd never asked. I'd never admitted that I questioned my relationship with God. I knew the time had come to answer my own questions. I spoke out loud again, this time in a voice that was surprisingly calm: "OK God, here's my body. If you want to use it, that's fine, but never again will I make excuses for your absence. If you're there, OK, but if you're not there, I will accept that."

It became clear in that moment that I had allowed my life to be controlled by circumstances. I never considered consciously that I had the power within me to guide my own existence. This was a very definitive moment for me. It became apparent that I didn't have anything to teach. So I decided to become a learner, and that I would be willing to learn from anyone – male or female, rich or poor, drunk or sober, young or old.

Just moments after my rage burst in the car, one of the tires went flat. As I was fixing it, a man – obviously drunk – walked up to me and asked if I could spare a quarter. I told him I had no money but that I could give him a ride to town. The situation, according to my training, begged for me to tell him how he could be "saved." Instead, I chose to find out if I could learn from the situation. I asked him what it was like to be drunk.

Tears started pouring down his cheeks and he proceeded to tell me his life story. I just listened. As I was dropping him off, he asked if he could come and talk to me sometime. His request floored me! I hadn't done anything for him except to ask a question and listen. This was quite the opposite of the response I received when I "witnessed."

I realized that it was time to give up the idea that I knew what everyone else needed. By choosing to learn, I provided a new context for bringing people into my life in a positive way. Feeling satisfaction and amazement, I started to look deeper inside for answers. I said to myself, "Paul, you've created a big mess. Anyone who can create this big of a mess must be powerful." So I asked myself how I could redirect this power to create joy rather than misery. I was feeling a shift.

A paraphrased passage from the Book of Genesis came to mind: "The seed brings forth the fruit of its own kind." The seeds I had been planting in my mind were failure and suffering, so that's what grew! I was creating my day, every day. All I could think about were my failures. Those thoughts produced more thoughts of failure which produced more failure. It was my creation, pure and simple.

So what would happen, I wondered, if I planted different seeds? I asked: "Paul, what thought, if held in consciousness, would you want to live with every day?" Another Bible verse came to mind: "I can do all things through Christ who strengthens me." I repeated it several times. Although I didn't fully understand, in that moment I started changing my pattern of thought. All I really knew was that something was helping me let go of the dark thoughts. It felt as if I were planting different seeds.

I incorporated the phrase into my life. I wrote the passage on several pieces of paper. I taped one on my bathroom mirror, I taped one to the sun visor in my car, and I kept one in my wallet. Every morning as I looked into the mirror I repeated the words. Again and again throughout the day, when I felt myself slipping, I repeated them. For me the words expressed a statement of my intention that I would no longer turn my power over to outside influences and to the fears residing in my mind.

I repeated the phrase in a conscious effort. Some days the words turned over and over in my head for hours. I was like a basketball player who shoots free throws over and over again. I started retraining my mind. It needed lots of practice.

Some days I grew tired of the drill. Doubts began to surface. But I knew that if I stopped practicing, my mind would do what I had conditioned it to do – descend into darkness and grow the thoughts of failure. That alternative was no longer acceptable. I couldn't stand who I had become. Without significant change I knew I would live out my life as a bitter person, certain of failure.

With that understanding it was not difficult to turn my thoughts back to that simple sentence. Even though I didn't know what I was going to do, I held onto the words.

That Sunday in church I knew I couldn't talk about faith or salvation or prayer. None of those concepts were real to me. So I decided to talk about what I could be honest about. It was frightening. I wasn't sure what would be an honest expression. So, instead of a typical sermon based on a biblical text, I named each person who was in church and shared what contribution he or she had made in my life. To my surprise, the response was overwhelming. Afterward one of the men said to me: "I don't know what's gotten into you, but whatever it is, don't stop!"

It was then that I recalled why we went to Mississippi in the first place – to be of service. I set out my intention to perform work that allowed me to feel I was being of service – whatever form it would take.

To my amazement, the circumstances of my life responded to my intention very quickly. Within two weeks the same religious organization that originally sent me to Mississippi wanted me to provide support to men who were in alternative service to the military and were working in civilian public service positions. My territory would be Kansas, Colorado, Nebraska and South Dakota. I could live anywhere in the region. I called Helen, told her I had accepted the position and by the next evening I was driving to Denver. Was it a miracle? It certainly appeared to be.

By setting forth my intention I began to follow my own heart. By trusting my thoughts and my desires I started the process of learning to trust my spirit. And I started learning perhaps the most important lesson of all – that my spirit is the divine expression of God.

The Mississippi experience was an awakening for me. By making the decision to leave, I started choosing the context of my life. I started creating my own circumstances and trusting my own inner wisdom to lead me. By acknowledging my own power, I began to replace self-hate with self-love. And, to my surprise, I felt myself free to love others more than I ever had before. The events of my life started shaping themselves to the context I chose.

If you were wondering about that money I'd borrowed in Mississippi: I made a commitment to myself that the $10,000 would be repaid, and it was – 23 years later! By that time principal and interest had grown to a total of $30,000 –

and that money put two of my creditors' kids through college! I could have viewed that debt as a chain dragging me down, limiting everything in my life. Certainly, I didn't enjoy it. Yet I came to view it as an opportunity to practice what I started learning during my days in Mississippi.

For more than 15,000 days since then I've been practicing – and it is much easier to see the joy in all things that are happening each day. Now, in my 74th year, I continue to set my intention and to create my circumstances every day. It has been a fantastic journey and more fun than I ever could have imagined. Now, I recognize that suffering is not something to be endured. Rather, it provides a signal that I am off my spiritual course. I know that each day I am bringing my behavior into alignment with the perfection of spirit.

I talk with hundreds of people each year, some of whom come to me for counseling. It is easy for me to recognize their perfection. Yet most people can't recognize it within themselves. They think of themselves as flawed and deserving of suffering, rather than as spiritual beings who are continually learning to express their perfection.

Planting Your Thoughts

Thoughts are seeds from which circumstances
grow after their own kind.

P.H.H.

Growing up in western Kansas I spent much of my youth working on the family farm or for other ranchers and farmers. Nearly every day I saw how the soil, when well tended, would produce crops for our communities.

We tilled and fertilized, and did everything we could to help it hold water. We gave it our attention because we knew it would produce crops, and those crops would become food to eat or products to sell. By tending the soil, we had jobs that produced income for our families. We cared for the soil, and in turn, it cared for us.

Throughout the centuries "tending the garden" has been used as a down-to-earth metaphor to describe the human condition. Some think it's been overused, some think applying the metaphor to human behavior is trite and overly simplistic. I like it because it is so beautifully uncomplicated.

Some of the statements I hear over and over again are: "It's a complex world and it's getting more complex all the time;" or "It's not that simple;" or "You're just naive if you think things can be that easy." Well, I give thanks that I am so naive.

To me the mind is a garden where we sow thoughts from which we harvest our experience of life. When we nourish our garden with tenderness and joy, it produces a crop that is loving and full of peace. When we feed our mind negative thoughts it produces sadness, anger and depression.

When a farmer plants corn, he doesn't think, "I wonder what will grow from these seeds?" He expects corn to grow. When I make a habit of consciously choosing the thoughts of love, joy and appreciation each day, then life begins to unfold accordingly as surely as corn follows the planting of corn seed. Our negative thoughts also produce negative experiences.

Have you ever tried to figure out how many positive thoughts you have in a day and how many negative thoughts you have? It's been estimated that the mind can produce thousands of thoughts every hour. The mind is so powerful that we can literally produce hundreds of thousands of thoughts in any given day.

Most thoughts are fleeting, they just blow through our minds like seeds in the wind. Others we hold and are planted.

With our linear consciousness we can hold just one thought at a time.

The question then becomes: How do you tell the difference between the thoughts that should be planted and the thoughts that should be allowed to blow past? It should be easy. The thoughts that allow us to feel free and joyful are those that should be planted. Those that make us feel tense and fearful are negative and should be allowed to pass. Thoughts that are good for us feel good, and those that aren't make us feel uncomfortable or bad.

For most of us, it's not that easy. We allow our thoughts to become confused. Let's take an example. What do you think about on your drive to work each day?

It might go something like this: "Running late. Should I go to 2nd Street to try to avoid traffic? No, it'll be packed. Don't want to be late. I'm gonna get ripped for that report. Got to pass this car. Too slow. C'mon, what's the hold up? The light's green, people! Need a cup of coffee. Can't forget Tammy's soccer practice, have to pick her up at 4:30 p.m. Oh, forgot her shoes! Damn. Have to run home at lunch. Lunch scheduled with Charley. Arrghh. Should get a car phone. Stupid morning radio talk show. I can't believe those politicians are doing this again! Oh, not a train! Why can't they get these tracks moved out of town? Whose idea was this morning meeting? I'm worried about making that down payment."

And that's all within the first two minutes of the drive! Most of the time our minds behave like one big run-on sentence!

You might say, "Oh, those aren't negative thoughts. It's just what's going on at the moment. Those don't matter." In my experience all those thoughts do matter. In fact, going back to the garden metaphor, a few years ago I thought it would be neat to plant my vegetables in circular patterns. To do that I first had to visualize what the garden would look like. It was a conscious decision. Several weeks after planting, the garden came up just as expected, in a circle.

So let's look back at the morning drive to work. What if the thoughts were planted like this: "I'll get to work in plenty of time for a productive day. The meeting can start without me. I'll be there soon enough. It will be interesting to learn what people thought of my report. Traffic is moving slowly, no problem. Gives me a chance to get centered and sort my thoughts for the meeting. It will be nice to pick up Tammy for soccer practice. Uh oh, I forgot her shoes. Well, she'll be fine in her tennis shoes for one practice. Looking forward to lunch with Charlie. Think I'll turn the radio off. It can be nice and quiet in the car in the morning. A train; I'll make some notes about how I'll make that down payment."

The first example seemed like driving back and forth across a field at high speed with no purpose. In the second example, I used the same subjects, but framed them in a different way. To do that I chose an image of tending soft, fertile soil. I planted calmness. I decided on a vision of what I wanted for the day. Our thoughts should guide us toward freedom, not restrictions. When I look back over the two examples, I get a tense feeling from the first. But in the second, I feel peace because I chose to plant the seeds of peace.

Think of the farmer who is driving around his fields in the spring. The ground is brown, the fields are bare. But what is he thinking about as he drives? He's not saying, "Oh, look at this dry dirt, what could possibly grow in this?" He knows what can grow in the field, and in his mind he sees tall crops, healthy and green.

If we dissected a brain, then cut out a small piece, then removed one cell, then examined the atomic structure of that cell, what would we find? That the most basic material of the brain is no different than the most basic elements of the soil.

Just as the farmer plants the seeds and nurtures the soil, you can plant the thoughts that nourish your mind. It does, however, require a mindful and conscious effort.

I once worked with a man who was an alcoholic. He was having difficulty in all aspects of his life. At one point he got drunk, jumped into a lake late at night and swam far out, apparently trying to commit suicide. He failed in his attempt by swimming back to shore. The next day he didn't remember what happened, but he knew something went wrong. So we had some sessions and I talked to him at length about what kind of thoughts he planted.

One day he went alone to a cabin in the mountains with the intention of planting positive, loving thoughts. The next morning he called me. "Paul, I tried it and it didn't work." "What didn't work?" I replied. "You said that if I planted good thoughts my circumstances would change. I spent the whole day changing my thoughts, but I'm still in the same mess I was in yesterday. It doesn't work!" he stated indignantly. I couldn't help but laugh. "Tom, do you know what you did? You planted your radishes yesterday and then dug them up today to see if they were growing. Everyone knows that seeds need time to germinate, and that seeds planted today won't appear as plants tomorrow."

Thoughts produce thoughts after their own kind. And thoughts produce our experiences in life after their own kind. Many of us have spent a lifetime in negative thought, so our brains are fertile for more unproductive thoughts.

Many years ago I thought I was doing a pretty good job planting my thoughts, but I continued to struggle with some things in my life. I was having a hard time changing some aspects of my thinking. I talked about it with a man who had written an article in which he explained that we reap what we sow. When I told him what was happening, he asked me a couple of questions.

He started, "Paul, how long have you been planting those negative thoughts?" "Oh, quite a few years…basically my whole life," I replied. "Well, you still have a crop to reap," he informed me. "You've got to let the old cycle play out while you're planting your new seeds." He was right. Sometimes it takes years to identify all the negative seeds we have planted and change them to the ones we want.

Another example of this was when I was presenting a talk to inmates in the county jail, explaining how thought is the seed for action. There were 14 men and one woman in the group. Everyone listened quietly for about an hour. Then suddenly the woman just burst out, "Look, I work hard all week. If I want to go out and do drugs on Friday or Saturday nights, that's my business." My answer was easy. "If you keep thinking the way you are thinking now, your life will keep working the way it is now. If that's OK with you, that's OK with me." The men just burst out laughing. Here she was sitting in jail wearing orange coveralls! I'm sorry to say she never grasped what I was talking about, but what a perfect example of planting negative thoughts.

Her case seems rather extreme, but all of us have fallen into the trap of imprisoning ourselves with our thoughts. A thought is a seed from which circumstances grow. If you say "I can't," or "I won't," or "I should," what will grow from those thoughts? Scarcity, despondence, surrender. If you say "I can," or "I will," or "I choose," what will grow from those thoughts? Something that's a lot better and a whole lot more fun...*homemade joy!* So how long does it take to harvest the wonderful bounty of loving, positive thoughts? Some people can turn their thoughts around overnight. And while everyone is capable of making a major shift very quickly, few of us make the change so fast. So be patient and treat yourself with kindness as you begin to replant.

Over the years, through personal experience, through talking with others, and in my reading, I've found much evidence that significant changes can be made within a relatively short time. It seems that it takes about two weeks from the time the head owns it until the heart owns it. In other words, from the time the thought is planted until the time it begins to grow and take root.

That seems pretty reasonable to me, but here's the key. Your mind produces thousands of thoughts each day, but it is only those thoughts that you choose to hold in consciousness that are planted...those thoughts that you think over and over.

To plant your new seeds you might need to sit down every day and write in a journal about what you want in your life. You might meditate on a single clarifying thought for a few minutes each day. You might need to post notes around your house to give yourself reminders. You might close your eyes at work for a few seconds each day to quiet your mind and allow those racing thoughts an opportunity to pass.

I like to remind myself of who I am when I am truly being who I am. This passage from the Bible is my reminder: "...the fruit of spirit is love, joy, peace, patience, gentleness, goodness, kindness, faithfulness and self-control."

Whatever you do, it will require a conscious effort to choose your thoughts at any point in time. It is a conscious effort that reveals the negative thoughts that are incompatible with your spirit. So it requires constant attention to plant the thoughts that serve spirit. Remember that loving, peaceful thoughts are the natural way of spirit. You know when your peaceful thoughts are interrupted. The power is within you to recognize that frame of mind and change it.

This doesn't mean that you should try to disregard the difficult situations you face. Quite the contrary. Remember the example of driving to work? Your thoughts can be reframed and planted in the soil of spirit instead of the soil of ego. The question, then, is this: What do you want to plant? If you want fear and anger in your life, plant the seeds of resentment and discontent. But if you want joy and satisfaction, plant the seeds of peace, love and understanding.

Choosing Your Container

Energy is best spent choosing the container rather than trying to arrange the content.

P.H.H.

On several different occasions during my life I attempted to provide income for my family working as a salesman. A pattern repeated itself in my sales experience. In the initial phase I was quite successful. My sales manager thought that he had really found a winner. Then after a couple of months my sales would drop off to almost nothing. One day it dawned on me that I was trying to be a successful salesman while unconsciously holding the expectation of failure. Eventually I discovered how I was sabotaging myself by using the following metaphor.

Let's say that every memory and every event in your life is represented by a marble, and that you must carry the marbles everywhere you go. Of course, if you don't, people will realize that you have "lost your marbles." The only way to carry all those marbles is to put them in something. If you put them in a sack, they will take the shape of the sack. If you put them in a box, they will take the shape of the box. If you put them in a container that's shaped like a duck, will they take the shape of a duck? Certainly. They'll always take the shape of the container. And if you have so many marbles you need to put them into several ducks, I would suggest you put them in a row.

If you want the events of your life to take the shape you desire, put your energy into choosing the container. The container, or context of your life, is created by the deepest desires and expectations you hold. Thoughts produce thoughts after their own kind. If you hold thoughts of fear, fear will hold power over you. If you hold thoughts of joy, happiness and peacefulness, those are what will influence your life.

Unfortunately, most of us are cautious of lofty, joyful thoughts. We're afraid of them because we've been conditioned to believe that our best thoughts are not realistic. We have lost sight of the fact that all true creativity takes us beyond what is, to what might be. When joyful thoughts come up we usually discount them. If it seems too good to be true, it probably is. We say, "Look at the mess I am in.

Look at all the problems in my life. How can I walk around feeling good?"

Well, who said that thoughts of fear, loneliness and despair are the most natural or the most realistic? Thoughts held in consciousness, no matter how mundane or how profound, are what provide the daily context of our lives. What I choose determines what I see in others and in myself.

Every morning I get to make a choice. I can decide what I want to be and what I want for the day. I deliberately choose what I will be first, then I think about what I will do. I like to say that I choose my "beingness" before I choose my "doingness." By choosing my "beingness" I create a daily container for what I want to experience that day.

And what is it that people want every day? Most people want to be happy and fulfilled in their lives. Most people want to express their love in giving and receiving. People don't wake up and say, "I really want to have a lousy day. I want it to stress me out. I want people to be difficult."

Yet, what do most of us do? Our behavior is rooted in our language, our thoughts, and our expectations. People drag themselves out of bed and focus on everything they must do that day. They focus on the people they must deal with and the decisions they will have to make. They focus on the doingness. And that can create a context for disaster, or at least a day that's not very pleasant.

By focusing first on what you have to do, you allow the events of the day to control your life. You focus on the external, the doingness. It gets even worse if you know you will be facing something that is not very pleasant.

Each day, the first thing I do is to make a choice of who I am and how I want to be, to set the context for my day. It's all part of the routine I started for myself more than 40 years ago. As soon as I wake up I begin the process of choosing my container. Every morning as I step into the shower, I say to myself: "I choose to be love and joy, peace and patience, gentleness and goodness, kindness and faithfulness, and in control of self." Throughout the day, as I encounter various situations, I remind myself again of who I am.

When I first started this morning exercise, I felt dishonest. Yet, I knew that those words held the essence of who I am, of my truth. I recognize there are many times when I act out of false impressions of who I am, but I can always choose to return to my truth by returning to my "beingness." What I choose to be determines what I see in others and myself.

Each day I am confronted with situations that some people might consider less than ideal. I might spend hours with someone who is experiencing a personal loss. Frequently, I'm called out to talk with someone who is contemplating suicide. I talk with couples experiencing conflict. And like everyone else, I have my own problems: my checking account is low; I need a car that starts; someone in my family is ill; the neighbor's cat is using my rose garden as a litter box.

There are two ways that I can look at these situations. Here's one way. "Boy, this is going to be a drag. What a pain. I'm tired of dealing with someone else's problems. There's never enough money...." So where is my focus? On the problems. I affirm the difficulties. The focus is on what I don't want to have in my life. It's easy to see how the day can become one big hassle. Then what follows? The brain – the ego – starts having a field day. "How did I get myself into this? Why me? I've got to get a better job. I've got to make more money. I've got to get a better relationship. Life isn't fair." All of those things are about doing. And they all help to plant the seeds of doubt. Points of misery, I like to call them.

Is misery what you want to choose? Each day you get to decide on the container that will package all of your events. So you might say, "I hate my job," or, "This stinks." Then all the events of the day will take the shape of the container you've chosen.

There is another way. What if the containers you choose daily are love, happiness and peace? What would those containers look like? How would they feel? How would they shape the events of the day?

Your energy flows freely when you choose the context, not the content! You are at peace and centered when you decide who you are and what you want to experience.

You might be thinking. "Paul, you've had a lifetime to work on this. And besides, you don't know about the idiot I have for a boss. You don't know about my work deadlines. You don't know how much money I owe on my credit cards." No, I don't know your circumstances, but I do know this. If you keep looking at what is not working, the same pattern will repeat over and over again.

A close friend and I talked about this. She is a nurse. She loves people and healing, but she absolutely dreaded the paperwork. Those tasks took away from what she truly loved. So where did she put her focus? On the paperwork. The container she chose took the shape of what she dreaded. It made her angry. She began to doubt her love of people and of nursing. Eventually, she quit.

When the seeds of doubt are planted, everything else grows around them. It is like tending the weeds instead of the flowers in the garden. You feel like a failure, you feel that you can't accomplish what you want, and you're too scared to change. It cycles and becomes a swirl from which there seems no escape.

I was working with a couple who were arguing over whether to declare bankruptcy. They were only $2,000 in debt. He wanted to declare, she didn't. I asked him, "If you could imagine having anything you wanted out of this, what would it be?" "I want all of our creditors to be accepting of this bankruptcy," he answered. I was surprised. "I asked you to imagine having *anything* you want. Why couldn't you imagine that you have the money to pay them?" He looked at me, confused, and said, "Well, I guess I never thought of that." Isn't that incredible! He felt so trapped by one thought. Yet, it's the way many of us think because we can't imagine our lives being any other way.

Is there a difference in the container he used to shape his thoughts and the container you use for the difficult situations in your life? Do you believe you are trapped by circumstances? Do you believe you are incapable of choosing your container?

You have the power to purposefully choose your beingness. You have the power to choose who and how you want to be. You have the choice to start each day by selecting your container. You can change your thoughts from choosing to see what isn't working…to seeing what there is to learn from the situation."

When something comes up that's tough, it's easy to affirm, "This is a drag. I hate this," but instead of reacting with loathing, you can choose a different container. Instead of thinking, "I hate this" 20 times a day, you can think: "Everything that happens today is an opportunity to learn something." At first this might feel contradictory to your thought process. We've all been taught that we must see problems as negative, but is that what you want?

When I'm headed into a meeting that I know will be difficult, I have choices. I could say, "This is gonna be a drag." But what I say to myself is this: "Everything that happens today is in the best interest of all concerned and I choose to see through the eyes of love and appreciation." Even when your boss is unreasonable, even when your partner is difficult, even when someone cuts you off in traffic, when you choose the container of love and patience you'll understand that what someone else is "doing" can't change what you have decided to be.

What if you choose to see hope instead of despair? What if instead of hating yourself for something you did yesterday or a long time ago, you love yourself knowing that you did the best you could at the time? What if you decide on a different container from this day forward? And what if you choose to honor your old thoughts, then let them die?

Over the years I've sought ways to help me select my container. One of my favorites is to read the prayer of St. Francis of Assisi.

Lord (I am) an instrument of thy peace.
Where there is hatred, let me sow love;
Where there is injury, pardon;
Where there is doubt, faith;
Where there is despair, hope;
Where there is darkness, light;
Where there is sadness, joy.
Oh divine master,

Grant that I may not so much seek to be consoled,
    as to console;
To be understood, as to understand;
To be loved, as to love.
For it is in giving that we receive;
It is in pardoning that we are pardoned;
And it is in dying that we are born to eternal life.

Simplify and Clarify

The most useful ideas simplify and clarify.

P.H.H.

I live about halfway between Denver, Colorado, and Cheyenne, Wyoming. Most times when I leave town, I travel south to Denver. One day I was supposed to go to Cheyenne. I got in the car and started driving. After about half an hour I looked at an exit sign and realized I was heading towards Denver. I laughed. It was out of habit that once I got in the car I automatically drove south. So I got off at the exit and turned back north.

So you ask, "Big deal, what else could you have done?"

Well, I could have kept on driving. I could have questioned and analyzed and criticized myself for what had gone wrong: "Boy, that sure was stupid. What was I thinking about? What did my parents do to me to make me take the wrong road? There must be something I'm trying to avoid. There is a deeper meaning to this." If this sounds ridiculous, it is. Most things in our lives need correction, not analysis.

If you had been driving, I'm sure you would have done exactly the same thing I did. "OOPS, going in the wrong direction, better turn around now. No reason to travel another foot further." Simple as that.

So, why can't we do the same thing when it comes to our own life? When we recognize that we are off track in our journey, and most of us can, what prevents us from adjusting our course? It is because we turn away from listening to our own inner voice, our spirit. We refuse to trust what we know in our hearts.

Seeking happiness is not something that needs to be delayed until you learn more about what doesn't work! I didn't need to learn more about heading in the wrong direction in the car. I didn't need to know how fast I was going, or how many miles out of the way I'd gone, or how long it had taken me to get there. I just needed to turn around. I knew I wasn't headed in the right direction.

In my work over the years, I've found that most people who are seeking happiness try to make this idea of turning around very complicated. People insist on deep analysis, on questioning their motivations and trying to figure it all out. Certainly there's nothing wrong with examining your life. I look at mine each day.

Yet, what happens is that many of us use that analysis to chain ourselves to the past. We believe we possess some sort of flaw. We believe that there is something about ourselves that we must fix. We are paralyzed to move from analysis to action. What we fail to recognize is that there is nothing fundamentally wrong. There is nothing to fix.

I see a lot of people who are depressed. I'm always amazed when they come in to see me and say, "I have this wonderful therapist who has given me such insight into my depression." And I say, "Fantastic! That means you're over your depression." And they say, "Well, no." "So tell me something," I ask, "If you're not over the depression, what good are all of these insights?"

Sometimes I get in trouble when I talk about this. People think I'm discounting psychotherapy. I'm not. My concern is that people get into therapy or they begin self-analysis to search for their flaws. They look for what's wrong. In the beginning that is appropriate, but only to the extent that it clarifies what they want. Then the focus needs to shift to how life will be when it's working. Many people get stuck looking for problems and forget about why they started the search in the first place – to live life joyfully.

Most of us know what we don't want, and that's where many of us place our focus. That is where we are stuck. Our energy flows toward what we think, speak and give our attention to. That's why so often we get what we don't want. People come to me and say, "Paul, I've got all these things that I don't want." "So what *do* you want?" I'll ask. And the answer I receive in too many cases is: "I don't know."

To get a new pair of pants requires a conscious effort. First you look in your closet and decide that what you have is old, does not fit anymore or is out of style. In other words, you identify the problem. You decide you need a new pair of pants. You go to a store and find the right size in something you like, try them on, and pay for them.

To find what you want in life requires exactly the same thing – consciously going from what you don't want any more to what you do want. It takes more than identifying what you don't want. You must give your attention to what you do want. And that is something you can do right now!

In my counseling, I have been criticized for not giving enough attention to problems. It has been my experience that people fall into the trap of blaming parents, teachers, politicians, siblings, bosses, co-workers, police, or anyone else who is handy. When you place the blame on someone else you give away your own power. All frustration centers around a sense of powerlessness. If you believe you are powerless you will not get what you want in life.

It's appropriate to look at where you've been, but spend as little time as possible there. Of much greater value is deciding where you are going. That is where your focus must be if you want joy, peace and fulfillment in your life. When you focus attention on what you want, that is where your energy will flow.

If each time a weed came up in your garden and you spent all of your time trying to figure out where it came from, how much gardening would you get done? When a weed comes up, you pull it, or hoe it, or spray it. You get rid of it and don't give it a second thought.

You don't want the weed. You don't need the weed. What you want is a garden that is full of wonderful vegetables. You know that with a bunch of weeds in the garden the vegetables won't grow the way you want them to. So why do we spend so much time analyzing and re-analyzing our own weeds?

A favorite hobby of mine is finding the original meaning of words. One of the words in our language that carries so much weight is "sin." The meaning we've assigned to it is of evil, of doing wrong. During the Middle Ages, sin was a term used by archers. Their assistants would stand near the target and signal where the arrow hit. If it was off the mark, the assistants would yell, "Sin!" Upon hearing that the archers didn't go off into the woods and analyze what went wrong. They didn't condemn themselves. To the archers it meant, "Get another arrow." "Sin!" simply meant that the shot was off the mark. So the archers adjusted and tried again.

Some of your shots in life are not going to hit the bull's-eye. But you don't have to spend time worrying about the things you tried that didn't work. All you need to do is respond to your desire to feel joy, to feel your true spirit. You know when your arrow is off the mark. You know when you're going in the wrong direction.

I know when I'm not happy, so I choose to adjust. Not because I've recognized some flaw in my character, but because I know how it feels in my heart. I create the best environment around me when I feel good. My body works best when I feel good. My relationships work best when I feel good. I'm at my most creative when I feel good.

When I feel good, I know I am following spirit. Yet I know so many people who won't allow themselves to plant that joy. They choose to look past it to what is next. "Well, it's going pretty good now, but just wait. Something is going to go wrong. It always does." Then what happens? Something goes wrong. The seed has been planted. There is nothing wrong with just feeling good. And a brief moment in time is all it takes to plant that seed and allow it to start growing. All you need to do is choose not to go one inch further when you know you're not going in the direction of your joy. Don't go to Denver when you want to go to Cheyenne.

To paraphrase a friend of mine: There is no such thing as a miserable journey to a happy ending. If you choose, you can turn your life around...right now!

Our Internal Navigation System

The guide within is one voice. The many
on the outside confuse us.

P.H.H.

Our son-in-law is an airline pilot. When he is preparing to depart from an airport, he enters their flight plan into the computerized navigation system. The computer constantly checks the position of the plane to the flight plan and indicates where the plane is in relation to that plan. When the navigation system indicates that the plane is off course, the pilot has to decide whether or not to make an adjustment in the course. There are times, due to weather or traffic conditions, when the pilot might choose to depart from the original plan. It is important to note that the computer does not say, "Hey, stupid, you are off course." The pilot doesn't curse the computer for giving him the information, nor does he curse himself for being off course. The messages are information from the computer to help him determine whether to enter an adjusted flight plan or get back on the original course. Each of us has an internal guidance system somewhat like the navigation system in the airplane. We have "negative" feelings and "positive" feelings. Our negative feelings tell us when we are off course and our positive feelings tell us when we are aligned with our spirit. Negative feelings leave us with a feeling of dis-ease; positive feelings give us a sense of well-being – being well.

Quite often I am asked, "Is it wrong to get angry?" A more helpful question would be, "What is this anger trying to tell me?" Typically, people who are fearful and resentful become angry. They want to "get even" with someone else, or they want to defend their actions, or they want to prove that they are right. All the defense mechanisms engage, the ego comes storming out, and people are consumed by the emotion. Anger becomes embedded in our personality and is expressed as despair, depression and aggression.

What we forget is that everyone has a choice about their anger. Anger is our inner guide telling us that we are off course. Most of us don't like to be angry. It doesn't make us feel good. Still, too often we let it strangle us. Anger is the emotion we feel when we believe we've tried everything and nothing works. It is born out of frustration. It develops in relationships, at work or in reaction to the injustices of the world. For some people the roots are much deeper, resulting from childhood wounds that are not recognized until well into adulthood.

I don't believe in telling people, "Don't get angry." We should be profoundly grateful that we have emotions. People who don't have strong negative emotions usually cannot have strong positive emotions. But it is important that we recognize what anger really is: a signal that tells us we're disconnected from our purpose.

It provides a clear signal. We need to learn that it is only a signal, not something that must consume us. Anger is not our natural condition, but it does provide a sense of direction. I am thankful for this and other negative emotions. I am off course in my spiritual journey more than I like to admit. There is nothing wrong with that. Negative emotion provides only one component of the personal guidance system.

So how does this relate to being mad at your boss? Anger provides information. Anger provides a signal that you are disconnected from your spirit. Just as joy provides the signal that you are on your spiritual path, anger shows you are off course. The anger is not making a judgment, it is simply providing a message. Just as the pilot trusts the plane's computer, we must learn to trust our own internal navigation system to lead us back to our true course.

Each of us wants to have a satisfying and complete experience of life, but at times we get caught up in all the anxieties, fears and vulnerabilities of being human. We are pulled off course. Life does not work the way we think it should. Then comes the frustration. Then comes the anger. Then comes the depression.

Much of our anger is rooted in our cultural consciousness. We are taught about duty and conforming to society.

Those concepts emphasize a world of obligations, working to please others, striving for a bigger paycheck, and on and on. In our society, conformity dictates that we focus on what is important to other people or to institutions. Whenever our focus is outside of ourselves, we set ourselves up to experience frustration and anger.

The traditional concept of marriage is perhaps the best illustration of this. Women have been taught that it is their "duty" to honor their husbands. Consequently, many women sacrifice their own dreams, which often breeds resentment and frustration. Men are taught in a similar manner. No matter how miserable the marriage, it is the husband's "duty" to take care of his wife. Men and women respond by saying, "Well, that's life. That's just the way it is."

I can think of nothing more frustrating than simple resignation to circumstances! That's when people shut off their navigation systems, stuff their true feelings, and fall into anger and depression. What most of us are not taught is to love and trust our deepest inner feelings.

So how does this work? Imagine yourself in a situation that is less than ideal and in which you are feeling angry. The anger is a communication from your higher self, from your internal navigation system telling you something is not right.

It is at this moment when choices present themselves. In difficult situations you can choose to become resentful, plot revenge, scream at someone in another car, or allow the circumstances to burn a hole in your heart. Too often, we struggle with anger instead of allowing it to teach us, to provide us with information. There is another way. This is where you ask yourself: "What is this anger trying to tell me?"

The anger is your feelings telling you that the situation is taking you off course. When a plane is steered off course to avoid a storm, the pilot doesn't forget where the plane is supposed to land. Unfortunately, when anger takes hold, you often forget where you want to go. Then it appears that the circumstances are knocking you off course permanently.

It is possible to change. Every negative emotion is pointing you to what you really want. The anger is not something to struggle with, but rather something to help guide our course.

You can accept the anger as providing a point of navigation for your true spirit. You can say, "So this is what the anger is trying to tell me." Your true course is not frustration. It is not your true nature to condemn or to criticize yourself or others for being off course. When situations arise in your life that are difficult, view them only as what they truly are; information to help guide you.

If someone says or does something that makes us mad, we have choices. We can hold onto the anger and allow it to ruin our day, week or life. We all know people whose lives are controlled by anger.

The choice is ours. By trusting our inner guide, we can use difficult situations to remind us that the course we follow is the course of joy. And we can recognize that the negative emotion of anger is our spirit saying: "This isn't the path to try." As we practice using both positive and negative emotions as a guidance system, we become aware that we are drifting off course long before our situation is out of control. We can then make corrections accordingly.

As each of our four children learned to drive a car, it was interesting to notice how long it took before passengers in the car no longer swayed back and forth with each correction of the steering wheel. After a few days or weeks, the car still drifted off to the right or left, but the driver sensed the drift so quickly and made the correction so soon that the passengers were not aware that a correction had been made. It can be the same with our emotions and our life's direction!

Love or Fear

Perfect love casts out all fear.
JOHN 4:18

Back in the late 1950s I was talking to a friend who told me I should go back to college. "I know I should," I said, "but I can't." "What do you mean you can't?" he asked. Uncomfortable in discussing the subject, I said, "Well, it's none of your business, but I'll tell you anyway."

I explained to him that I'd lost a lot of money in a failed business venture, that I had a family to support, and that I just couldn't afford to go to college. He responded quickly: "What's that got to do with it? Do you want to go to college?" Believing that I hadn't provided enough detail, I started my explanation again, and with considerably more emphasis. There were four kids to feed, I owed $10,000, and my job paid only about $5,000 per year. We lived strictly month-to-month, pinching every penny. It would be impossible to find the money to pay tuition.

He was totally unimpressed. When I finished, he looked me right in the eye and asked: "But Paul, do you want to go to college?" Dumbfounded, I looked at him with some disbelief. It all seemed so simple to me – I just couldn't afford it. He spoke again: "Paul, that's not the way to make decisions. You make the decision about what you want first, then you figure out how. If you try to figure out how first, it will stop you every time." So he asked again: "Do you want to go to college?" He'd managed to chip a small crack in my mind set. I answered, "Yes," but without much conviction.

That conversation played over and over again in my mind. I needed months to grasp what he was saying. What he was explaining was the difference between choosing fear and choosing love.

In fear we express doubts, uncertainty, resistance; we are disconnected and blaming. In fear we attempt to figure out how, before we figure out what. We attempt to figure out all the details, and there are always hundreds. We sabotage our creativity and our inspiration. In love we express what is possible with confidence, knowing and trust. In love we identify what we want, and know that the "hows" will present themselves as the path unfolds.

My focus at the time my friend confronted me about school was generally on fear. I filled myself with uncertainty and frustration. I chose only to see that it would be impossible to go to school. I mulled that conversation over and over again in my mind. It took me another eight months to focus on what I wanted.

I wanted to study psychology. I found that a college about 120 miles south of where we were living in Texas offered an introductory class one night each week. So I called up and enrolled, even though I knew the drive would be difficult.

Good things happen when you let go of the "hows." I found out that four other people from my town were taking classes at the same school, so we were able to drive together and share the expense. One of the "hows" was taken care of even before the class started.

During that semester Helen and I also decided that we wanted to move back to Colorado. Six months later we were living in Colorado. I enrolled in classes at a nearby university and found a job that paid more and had a schedule that didn't interfere with school. Helen, who is a nurse, also discovered many job opportunities. We also found a wonderful home for our family.

Within five years I earned a degree, nearly paid off my debts from Mississippi, and started a career as a counselor. I became the first social worker in our school district, then became head of the county's probation office and later started my own counseling business. My family never went hungry and I was able to get loans and grants to pay my tuition.

What an amazing lesson! Often I am asked how to displace fears. So I tell that story.

Clearly, it is a matter of setting an intention. Once I decided to go to school, my full attention was given to that purpose. I shifted my focus to what I wanted, sparking my desire and my excitement. The "hows," the steps, unfolded as they were needed. And my fears? They faded with each new experience. By releasing the fear, I chose a different mode – love. And from that mode I expressed my joy and moved toward what I wanted.

That experience helped a colleague and me develop a couple of simple charts, designed to challenge people's belief systems. We used these in our counseling business. We attempted to identify those qualities which provide the context to make life joyful. We also identified the context which serves to disrupt our lives. I use the charts when I hear people tell me how hard their lives have become or how impossible they believe it is for them to change.

One of my early experiences using the charts was in a class for people who had received tickets for drunken driving. The class was not about showing people movies of bloody wrecks on the highway. It was about helping them explore their behaviors and motivations, and allowed them to decide if their behaviors were getting them what they wanted.

I displayed the following charts and explained that they could change their lives by applying these concepts every day.

Love Profile

Non-judgmental • Open • Compassionate
Honest • Appreciative • Caring • Considerate
Genuine • Responsible • Patient • Trustworthy
Trusting • Forgiving • Healthy • Joyful
Connected • At Ease

When I showed that chart to the class, the response was predictable. "Oh, that's nice Paul. But no one really lives that way. That's Pollyanna stuff." I answered, "Yeah, you're right. That is pretty idealistic. So let's look at the alternative." Then I brought out the second chart.

Fear Profile

Close-minded • Angry • Judgmental • Blaming
Inconsiderate • Greedy • Resentful • Hateful
Vengeful • Violent • Resistant • Critical
Dishonest • Isolated • Anxious • Separated
Prone to disease (dis-ease)
Disconnected • Alienated • Lonely • Insecure

Reading this, the classes usually fell silent. Most people saw plainly that their behaviors and attitudes reflected many of these qualities and had led to their arrests.

"So do these describe how you want to live? Will these get you what you want?" I inquired. During six years of classes in which I taught more than 2,000 students, I never once found anyone who didn't recognize that living in the fear profile doesn't work. In our culture fear is used as a motivator, but it never provides long-lasting effects. Fear as a motivator lasts only until you go to sleep because you have to – at least temporarily – let go of fear to sleep. It is love and joy that provides the true foundation for life.

The people in those classes faced the same types of challenges all of us face every day – jobs, bills, strained or broken relationships, life changes. They went out to a party or went to a bar in an attempt to make a connection, or to forget one. They used alcohol to enhance their mood or to find something they felt they lacked in their lives. By looking outside themselves for answers they became more disconnected, lonely and insecure.

It is not just people who attempt to find their joy in drugs and alcohol who live in the fear profile. Have you ever said, "Well, I'll just have to cope with it." We cope with our jobs, we cope with our partners, we cope with our kids, we cope with our lives. Coping keeps people in the fear profile. Coping is resignation to a life that is unsatisfactory, something to put up with, something that is merely tolerable. Resignation eventually leads to resentment and anger, isolation and depression.

It is our choice to decide that life is not an exercise in coping. To live fully and to express our true spirit is to ascend into love. Does it seem difficult at times when you are surrounded by people who are full of fear or anger? Certainly. But what is the alternative? You can choose to go to their level. You can drop into a coping mode. You can fill your life with resentment and anger. Or you can choose to acknowledge that at this moment you can make a different choice – a choice of love instead of fear. Love is natural, hate has to be learned.

I wrote the following poem for Valentine's Day and I use it often as an affirmation of life.

> *Love is like oil, hate is like sand.*
> *Love is uplifting, hate is depressing.*
> *Love opens, hate closes down.*
> *Love does not judge, hate holds us to our past.*
> *Love looks for what is lovable, hate looks for what*
> *   is mean.*

Love binds together, hate tears apart.
Love accepts, hate rejects.
Love makes for happiness, hate makes for sadness.
Hate appears as fear, resentment, grudges,
*   disgust, ugliness.*
Love appears as appreciation, forgiveness
*   and beauty.*
Love does not mean I must live with you.
*   It does mean I appreciate you.*
Love is a decision, not a hormone.

Thought Habits

We are what we think about all day long.
UNKNOWN

A friend of mine told me that she lived in fear of her husband's anger. Because of her beliefs, she felt paralyzed to do anything about it. She felt bound by tradition and expectation and totally discounted her need to seek joy. For ten years she believed herself to be a victim of circumstances over which she had no control.

Her husband was an alcoholic. As the misery became more overwhelming, she started looking more deeply at her situation. She knew her life was at stake. She checked into an Al-Anon program which assists people who live with alcoholics. During the course of that program, she had to face a major realization. She began to see that she was a willing participant in the whole process, and had lived that way for ten years.

After the program she continued to live with the man. One day, after one of her husband's tirades, she walked up to him, put her hand on his chest, and said to him in a very calm voice, "I am not afraid of you anymore." It was the first time she confronted him directly. Both of them knew right then that the relationship would never be the same. They divorced in less than a year. She related the story to me later and said that at the moment she confronted her husband she "felt like the most powerful person in the world."

Her power came from recognizing the needs of her own heart and listening to her spirit. She did not stop to consider all the steps that would be required to end the relationship. Instead, she listened to her inner wisdom and moved directly to what she wanted – her joy. Had she considered all the steps in between, she might still be in that marriage.

Deeply ingrained within all of us are belief systems that act as our guide. This guidance may manifest as a joyful spirit or as a demon. For too many of us, our belief systems pose as the demon, keeping us in anger, fear and frustration.

It is said that a belief is a thought that has been thought and accepted as truth over and over again. In our lives we receive many negative messages from every imaginable source. As those become ingrained we forget that our true source is spirit and the essence of our being is joy. We respond to the pain by holding on to our beliefs, even if they are part of the problem. A belief system – or B.S., as I like to call it – serves those ideas quite well and keeps us in our pain. A belief system is simply a group, set or collection of beliefs we hold about any person, place or thing.

Shifting out of our old belief systems could be the most important work of our lives, but it requires a willingness to let go of old ideas. For example, a phrase that I heard many times in my church experience: "Lord, I am not worthy." That statement sends a powerful message.

To shift that perspective, I now say: "Lord, yes I am worthy, deserving and entitled to all the joy and love that I desire." Now that has a different ring to it! When I say that, I feel good. I feel that I am a child of God, created in his image and likeness. Yet it took me years to truly believe that. It meant turning a belief system upside down, shaking down my ego and allowing new thoughts to plant their seeds.

In my life, the vast majority of the pain I have experienced has been because of my clinging to old ways. I believed that because I had learned something early in my life – consciously or not – that I had to hold onto it. I was convinced that because I held a belief it was right, and I was right, and everyone else should believe it was right. When I held on to those beliefs I found myself running into walls at every turn.

It was not until I let go of being ruled by friends, family and cultural consciousness that I could allow my spirit to lead. My heart did not engage its purpose until I released all of the "should haves" and the "ought tos." Only when I questioned my traditional thinking was I truly able to love and find joy. Holding on to an old belief system is holding on to the past. The past can provide valuable information, but that information must be examined and often released.

I am constantly amazed by the power that tradition and expectations hold over our ability to think for ourselves. A man who was married to an alcoholic complained to me that his wife treated the kids cruelly; she even beat them with wire hangers. In spite of that he felt obligated to hold the family together, to make sure that the kids grew up in a household with a mother and a father.

One day he brought his kids in to talk with me. Afterward I said to him, "Do you know that your kids don't know who their father is?" He was stunned. After a couple of moments he stammered, "What do you mean? I do everything for those kids. They know I love them."

"That might be true," I said, "but all I can tell you is what they told me. They don't know who you are because all they've ever seen you do is walk around on egg shells trying to keep from upsetting your wife." Maintaining the appearance of a traditional household blinded him to the fact that his children didn't see a family at all. He ended the relationship soon afterward.

That example is no different from what most of us play out in our mind every day. We worry, we regret, and we scold; all the time allowing our judgment and our fear to guide our thinking. That is not how God wants us to live. Spirit is not engaged in a belief system that produces fearful thoughts and action.

Our thoughts can shift to love. We can decide to forgive the old ways and then choose to allow the expression of our true and peaceful spirit. We can change our beliefs to recognize that in spirit we are free. We can live in a path of love that is true, not bow to the false gods of guilt, suffering, obligation, duty and expectation.

We are ruled by our old belief systems because we continue to give them attention. And what we give attention to grows. So it is time to give attention to spirit. Your inner being is not flawed; you are not destined to repeat some historical cycle. You are a perfect being created in the image and likeness of God. You only need to choose to be guided by spirit along the perfect path of joy and love.

Set a vision that describes the joy and the love you desire to have in your life right now. Don't consider "how" you're going to do that. Believe in what you desire and allow your spirit to fill your life with joy.

Here is an affirmation that I use to assist in shifting my belief systems. See if it works for you.

At this moment my journey is proceeding on the perfect course of love and joy. I am surrounded by people I love. My relationships are loving and safe, my work is satisfying, and I am guided by my perfect spirit. My beliefs allow contentment and help me explore my path without fear or doubt. As circumstances arise that appear difficult, I see them for exactly what they are: information from my spiritual guidance system.

I see how perfectly my path has evolved. Instead of worrying about how I am going to accomplish my goals, I only consider what those goals are and trust that as I give them attention they will be expressed in my life as I need them. I do not need to figure out "how," I only need to know "what." My mind is occupied with expres-

sions of perfection; my spirit accepts that I am willing to love; the doors open for me.

I choose to be guided by joy, not by tradition; I choose to be guided by joy, not by the expectations of others. I accept that it is God's intention for me to be happy, and that God expresses through my spirit perfectly. I let go of what is supposed to be. I trust and follow my inner guidance that always takes me to my contentment, my passion and my creation.

Do Butterflies Struggle?

How you define something determines how you behave toward it.

P.H.H.

A medical doctor and his children were exploring outdoors. They were on a hike and the kids found a board with three mud cocoons stuck to the back. They took the board home. A couple of days later one of the cocoons started breaking up on one end. Some large pieces fell off, but the hole was still mostly plugged by thin spikes of hard mud. The butterfly was attempting to get out.

They were all eager to see what would happen, so the father took his pen knife and cleared a passage for the butterfly. It was pushing to get out of the cocoon, so helping it a little seemed like the right thing to do. When the butterfly emerged they could see that it wasn't fully developed. It never flew and color never filled its wings. Within a couple of days it died. The father and his children saw that what they did to help actually deprived the butterfly of its chance to live.

The other two cocoons were left alone. The larvae inside appeared to be fighting to get out, but when they finally emerged they were beautiful. What seemed to be a struggle turned out to be an essential element of the butterflies' development. They needed that effort to gain strength and develop their basic life systems. The act of breaking out of the cocoon was not a "negative" experience for the butterflies.

I often hear parents talk about what they are going to do for their kids. Here is a typical statement: "I'm going to help my kids because I sure don't want them to struggle the way I did."

When parents say that I am fascinated by the word they use – "struggle." That is a word that is deeply rooted in our culture. It is synonymous with words like suffer, fight, battle, hard, and difficult.

We hear about how some people struggle to survive. We hear how people fight for their rights. We learn that every day is a battle in the competitive world. People say that they are "survivors." As a society, we have wars on drugs, crime and poverty.

That is very powerful language. It usually establishes a negative context or container for what happens. I wonder if there isn't a profoundly different way to look at what we commonly refer to as struggle.

In your attempt to "help" your child, are you stripping away the process of emerging? Are you really helping them when you finish their homework? What do they learn when you rescue them from hassles with friends or teachers? When they ask questions, do you give them the opportunity to answer it themselves? There is no need for children to be sheltered from challenges.

What about your interactions with others in your life? In intimate relationships it is not uncommon for one partner to rescue the other from some perceived peril or hurt. We have all observed a supervisor rescuing an employee, or one co-worker saving another from a struggle or problem.

What is actually the beautiful learning process of life is often referred to as a struggle. And because language is so powerful, it follows naturally for most of us that to achieve our goals in life we must experience battles, pain and hardship. Then we're told that after we've gone through all that pain and all those battles we're supposed to emerge joyous, happy and satisfied.

That just doesn't make any sense to me! I have a saying: "How you define it is how you behave towards it." If you refer to life's challenges as struggles, then a lot of life will look like a fight.

What is interesting about humans is that most of us spend our lives building our cocoons instead of breaking out of them. A question I get asked quite often is this: "How do we get into our messes? If we emerge from the pure positive energy that is God, then why all this mess?"

When we are children, we experience the flow of pure positive energy and we accept it without question. I suspect that most of us remember the feelings we had as children. And for most people there is a deep longing to return to a place of joy, where we feel a wholeness of being. As children we taste the glory and the preciousness of the universe.

But then we succumb to our beliefs regarding aging, sickness and death. As the negative experiences in our lives begin to affect us, we start building a new cocoon called "growing old." That cocoon appears to be very tough to break.

Other cocoons we spin are judgment of self and others. These cocoons are spun from fear and anger; from deeply rooted internal language that signals a continuing battle, a struggle. We lose track of the beauty that's inside. So instead of continually seeking the emerging path, we develop all kinds of systems to protect ourselves from feeling too much or loving too much. To lessen the pain we try drugs or alcohol. We try sex or TV or work.

Yet, at the same time, the voice of spirit continues to speak. It is the voice deep within that says, "I really want to be happy and express my love." Your deepest desire is to break out of the cocoons of the ego and social consciousness and emerge back into spirit. It is at precisely this point where many of us feel the most frustration.

The cocoon is usually well constructed. As you try to break out, the ego resists, building every challenge imaginable. There might be a divorce; you might get fired from your job; you might lose a lot of money or become ill or be rejected by your parents or children.

The question then becomes, how will you define the

process of growing and breaking free? Will you define it as the struggle of your life? Or will you define it as an emerging journey, knowing that you are moving toward free expression of spirit? How you define your emergence is how you will behave towards it. You do have a choice.

I remember an experience that Helen and I had when we were attending a training session at a Center for Attitudinal Healing in California. In one of our small group discussions, an AIDS patient spoke in a very positive manner about what he had learned through his illness. He explained that his big breakthrough came when he realized that he was not the disease. He learned that although the disease was carried in his body, it was not necessary to allow AIDS to affect his spirit. AIDS was his cocoon. He had to break out of that mud to find his true self, his perfect spirit.

Unfortunately, he had been condemned by his parents who were very ashamed that their son had AIDS. Yet, because he was so excited by what he was learning, he wanted to share his experience with his parents. So he went to their home for an extended visit.

When he arrived, he found that his parents had two big recliners set up in front of the TV set. His mother and father scheduled their days around what was on TV. Each of them had a favorite program for every hour of the day. They even ate their meals in front of the TV. "I was there for ten days and never got to talk to my parents," the man told our group. Now I ask you, who was in the cocoon and who was breaking free?

The parents criticized their son, however, they built a cocoon so tight that it was difficult for them to express or feel love. Yet their way of life, to some, is more acceptable than that of the man who has intentionally freed his spirit from a dying body.

His parents chose not to feel and they are trapped in their easy chairs. The son chose to allow his perfect spirit to emerge. Is your life a struggle or are you flying free?

Allowing the Path to Unfold

*Job descriptions are what you do until
the important things happen.*

P.H.H.

When I was head of probation for the county, the chief judge of our judicial district once asked me, "Where do you guys come up with all these ideas for helping kids to get out of their messes?" "I guess there are two answers to that question," I replied. "First, we are willing to take the one step that we can see without knowing what the next one will be. We take the first step based on the theory that if we are willing to take the first step the next one will reveal itself at the appropriate time. Secondly, we like to keep the 'monkey' on the right back by expecting the family to participate in figuring out what would be best for all concerned. It is truly amazing what creativity comes forth when we all share our ideas, and listen to the child who is at risk."

If we can believe that there is always a perfect path ready to unfold before us, and that there is an inner wisdom within each of us to recognize that path, then everything will present itself at the appropriate moment.

Yet our training usually inspires us to resist and to distrust. To trust the path as it unfolds appears to offer too much uncertainty – circumstances appear too difficult, or too easy. So we choose to plan our lives, forge a path and stick to it, no matter what. We believe that with enough planning or persistence everything will turn out the way we want.

I have found quite the opposite to be true. Planning, for some people, turns into an exercise of "shoulds" based completely on the expectations of family, friends or society. In considering the future, many people become paralyzed in perpetual analysis, unable to listen to their inner guidance. Planning then becomes a futile attempt to avoid any circumstance that appears to be unpleasant.

This is not to say that you should disregard the future, but rather to approach the future in a different way. Instead of making plans based on the expectations of society, friends and family, it is possible to be guided into the future by your inner wisdom – your perfect spirit. When you are centered in the spirit, your life is greatly simplified. You are an extension of God. You make decisions based on your joy, and what unfolds before you expresses divine perfection.

By making choices from your joy and integrity, you allow the path to unfold. Then it is possible to learn from life experiences, rather than worrying about making what some people refer to as "mistakes." We have all heard this phrase: "You learn from your mistakes." By referring to life experiences as mistakes, we discount our personal journey. When we convince ourselves that experiences are mistakes, too many of us become timid. We curse ourselves, wondering how we could have been so stupid and how we failed to see the "correct" answer.

A friend came into my office a few years ago to talk to me about a painful event in my life. He said, "You think of this experience as a failure, don't you? Why not think if it as an adventure?"

He was right, I had been looking at the experience as a mark against me rather than looking for something to be gained. We spend too much time trying to figure out how to avoid mistakes rather than embracing the wonderful experiences of life that serve to enrich our spirit. By choosing to avoid, we deny our essence; we deny our purpose as learning, growing beings.

Often we believe ourselves to be stuck deep in the mud. No matter where we turn we seem to sink deeper, and nothing appears available for us to hold on to. We thrash about looking for an answer or support. At times like this it is normal for people to look around and see only what they lack. It is "normal" for people to start comparing themselves to others and to pose questions that cannot be answered: "Why is everyone but me so happy? Why is everyone except me doing so well?"

If you feel that you are failing and begin comparing yourself to others, you are looking outside for answers that will never be found. It is only by accepting yourself with understanding, by looking within, and by allowing the path to emerge that you will find the source of your joy and happiness.

By comparing yourself to others and by judging your actions as mistakes, you fall into the trap of judgment, which only leads to more dissatisfaction. There is no reason to judge others and there is no reason to judge yourself.

Everything you do, all the circumstances of your life, are unfolding as the perfect path. I know it doesn't always look that way when you are in the middle of the muck. You have probably heard the saying: "When you are up to your rear end in alligators, it is hard to remember that your original intention was to drain the swamp." Most of the time situations appear to be negative only when you choose to see them that way. Our spirit does not view these situations as negative, only as experiences in which to gain greater understanding.

There were times when I attempted to plan my path. But along the way I learned that spirit holds little regard for the charted course. Spirit longs for freedom and light, not the straight and narrow trail.

During the late 1950s I accepted an invitation to be the leader of a church in the panhandle of Texas. With our memories of the difficult times we had just experienced in Mississippi still fresh, Helen and I both knew the move was risky. I felt confident however that I had grown. The possibility of experimenting with my ideas in a community over an extended period of time felt appealing. I also felt that I was most helpful working within the context of a church.

Before I accepted the position I made my intentions very clear to the leaders. One of the main issues I addressed was the idea of tradition. I explained that I would not seek to uphold any tradition for tradition's sake. I would only continue a tradition if it could be shown that it served a current and meaningful purpose.

This eventually caused some controversy within the congregation and within the regional hierarchy of the church. In less than a year I knew that it was time for me to leave. I felt compromised. I knew my integrity soon would be at stake and continuing as minister did not appear to be the best option.

The opportunity to leave came in the most unexpected way. A church of another denomination offered me a job directing its youth programs. I laughed when the offer was made, believing it would be impossible to go to work for another church in the same town. I never envisioned that sort of change, and it didn't appear to be part of the plan of going to Texas. Yet the new job offered what I wanted – a joyful and spiritual connection. I accepted the position.

With Helen's help, I recognized that the job offer was the path of spirit unfolding before me. Had I stayed in my original role I would have been trudging to the call of obligation.

When we listen to our spirit, the path unfolds before us. Most of us are taught to strive for control, to plot our future carefully and methodically. But we are constantly swept into the throes of change. When you are confronted by change, choices often appear difficult. At those times it is tempting to look outside for an answer. Those are the times

to look within, listen to your heart and be led by spirit.
When you respond to your joy, it doesn't matter what decision you make, the perfect path will unfold before you.

Seeking Significance

Everyone seeks significance in their own environment.
P.H.H.

"Everyone seeks significance in their own environment" is a simple statement I make to explain behavior. Whether you're the president or a first grader, you work to establish your sense of self and your place in the world. You have a unique perspective and your thoughts deserve to be heard.

Parenting is a good example. Parents want to make sure their children do the right things and don't harm themselves. They often feel that their children do not have the wisdom or the experience to make right decisions for themselves. So what happens far too often is that parents attempt to make most of the decisions for their children. If the decision-making process is taken away from the child, how does he or she learn to make wise decisions? How significant can a child feel who is only allowed to say "yes" to mom and dad. Who learns to say only what mom and dad want to hear? Usually parents will say, "As long as you live in this house, I'll make the decisions." When children are treated this way they'll be ill-equipped to make their own decisions and handle challenges they'll face later in life. Self-esteem is built into the process of making decisions and living with the consequences. Every normal child is reaching out for adulthood where they see themselves as free to make their own decisions and where their ideas are treated with respect.

I firmly believe that children should make every decision as long as they can fail and still live with the consequences. That allows children to seek their own significance and provides them a basis of understanding as they enter adulthood.

So how does this apply to adult relationships? In exactly the same way. To nurture and grow in our relationships, it is important to recognize the significance in every person we meet. By doing so we extend love, and in turn, that establishes trust.

I use five words to show how all of us seek significance in our own environment. I use the acronym CLURT to help people remember them: Curiosity, Limitations, Unexpected, Respect, and Tone.

CURIOSITY

Be curious about one another rather than interested in each other. Curiosity, by definition, is nonjudgmental. It seems as though everyone brings to a new relationship a set of expectations as to how that other person is supposed to look and behave. Some of our expectations are conscious and some are unconscious. In the early stages of most romantic relationships the fear of not meeting the expectation of the new partner makes us nervous and makes us want to keep our best foot forward. After the individuals get over the jitters of the first few dates, they are very curious as they learn about the new partner. Those early stages often feel very exciting. If we can keep that best foot forward, we fall in love...actually, we wade in.

As our relationships progress, it is typical that unfulfilled expectations begin to surface. Instead of asking questions to find out why the partner has come to see things the way they do, we seek to persuade or criticize in hopes that the partner will conform more closely to our expectations. For most people it is a natural part of the discovery process to determine if the relationship should continue. Yet, as relationships progress, we become manipulative in an attempt to make the other fit a preconceived notion of how that person should be.

This is also true of the parent and child relationship. At first the cute little baby is the pride of the parents' lives. That is, until the little one begins to assert his or her independence. Then pride begins to turn to criticism. To some people "train" means to force parental expectations upon the child.

Most parents say they want their children to talk to them. So a parent asks a question and the child gives an answer the parents don't like. Often, the response from the parent is,

"You shouldn't feel that way," or "why didn't you do this or that." The child feels criticized and thus diminished in his environment and then concludes, "I can't talk to my parents." Wouldn't it make more sense if the parent responded to answers that might be a bit disconcerting with, "Well, how did it work out?" or "If you had it to do over again, what would you do differently?" When parents inappropriately insert their opinions, they are expressing their own interests, not curiosity about their child.

When we listen with curiosity we accomplish two things that are absolutely profound. First, when we ask questions based in curiosity, we are imparting worth. We show that we want to know who the other person is. Second, when we ask someone questions that express curiosity, it gives that person permission to express her or his thoughts from beginning to end. It allows that person a feeling of significance. It provides that person unconditional permission to talk about his or her life without fear of judgment. Since we often do not think in complete sentences, it provides an opportunity for the person to complete their thought so that they themselves think it through more clearly.

Managers often express interest in employees rather than curiosity. Here is a typical question from the boss, "What is going on here? Why is this job late!" Clearly, that question expresses the self-interest of the boss. And the typical answer from an employee would be, "I'm working as fast as I can!" That statement is designed to get the boss off his back – not to communicate useful information.

But what if the boss expressed curiosity with a question like this: "What are your feelings about how that project is moving along?" That question gives the employee permission to provide more information, to explain any break-throughs or problems. Ultimately the boss gathers far more information and the employee feels that his or her position is valued. The same applies in all relationships. When you are not afraid of being judged, you will speak from the heart.

LIMITATIONS

If you have a job, you understand the types of decisions you can make as an employee. You know the limitations of your power. It is equally important to understand the limitations of your power in a relationship. You have only the power to guide a decision or to influence behavior. You can use force to temporarily change behavior and in the process create resentment. You cannot make decisions for someone else, or determine how someone is going to respond to what you say.

Many parents believe that their job is to make their kids "good." Well, they can't. Parents can only provide the environment in which the child can be good if he or she so chooses. Children learn by what they experience, not by what they are told.

In most close relationships, it is often the case that one partner will try to impose his or her views on the other. Many individuals feel it is their obligation to do so. By attempting to impose a view, you are acting from fear and dominance instead of love. Attempting to impose your will on another creates tension and resentment in a relationship, and tension creates an atmosphere that does not foster good decisions – certainly not good communication.

In relationships, your job is to recognize the significance of others, not to impose your values upon them. Your job is not to convince, but to seek information that reveals the strengths of the other person. Recognize what you have the power to do. Don't put your energy where you cannot succeed – even if it means ending a relationship.

UNEXPECTED

Too many of us allow our lives to become clichès. We talk in clichès, we act in clichès, we answer in clichès. We ask clichè questions: "How's it going?" "Did you have a good day at school?" "How was work?" And we get clichè answers: "Good." "It was OK." "Fine."

We can't always come up with a great question or a witty response. These are harmless responses when we can't engage in a conversation, but we allow these typical hollow questions to take over other aspects of our lives. We forget to give compliments, we forget to offer surprises, we lose our resolve to face situations with creativity and excitement. All too often, the clichès spread into our relationships and leave them flat.

When I was head of the county probation office I encouraged everyone to think creatively and independently. Sometimes that resulted in some uncomfortable situations.

One day a probation counselor I supervised marched over to the district attorney's office and chewed him out for the way he was handling a case. Before I knew what happened, the DA called me and said, "Do you know what Bill just did? He ripped me up one side and down the other." The DA expected me to be on the defensive, or to apologize and explain how I would reprimand the employee. Instead, I said this, "Apart from how he approached you, did he have a point?" That surprised the DA, who answered, "Well, yes he did." I said, "OK, so why don't we deal with that issue and I'll approach him later about how he talked to you."

Later, I said to Bill, "I think you have some qualities that you could get more mileage out of." "OK Paul," he said, "What did I do wrong?" "Well, I got a call from the DA's office today." Without further explanation, Bill said with some regret in his voice, "Oh Paul, I'll go over there and apologize." "I'm not asking you for that," I replied. I don't want you to stop being who you are. I want to talk about how we can get more mileage out of who you are."

The whole situation could have fallen into the clichè of perceived power. I could have responded to the DA by saying, "Yeah, I've been having a problem lately with Bill, I'll straighten him out." Then I could have called the employee on the carpet and reprimanded him for his behavior. But I knew that would only serve to shut down the creative thinking of people in my department. I knew that I would discourage Bill's feeling of significance if he knew that I was constantly looking over his shoulder.

Afterward, the DA and I exchanged important information that probably wouldn't have come to light if I had handled it with a clichè answer. The employee learned that his ideas were valued, and we also talked about how he could improve his approach.

We all know of similar situations that have occurred with our spouses, friends or children. The next time your kid "screws up" don't jump to the clichè response: "I told you never to...," or "If I told you once I told you a thousand times...," etc. Stop for a moment and consider what you could do to help yourself and your child learn more from the situation. Instead of asserting the false power of the clichè, use the true power of a question that is filled with curiosity.

With others, consider the power of the loving surprise. For example, a compliment that transcends the standard and expected response. A few years after I was married, my wife said to me, "Paul, I love the way you giggle when someone surprises you." Now that felt good!

RESPECT

A father brought his son into my office for a counseling session because the boy was not doing well in school. "No son of mine is going to flunk social studies," he pronounced. "Well, he just did," I said.

"So what do I do about it?" the father asked. I immediately turned to his son, "What's the best grade you made this last quarter?" "An A...and I made two this quarter," he answered. "How does it feel when you make an A?" I continued. "It feels great," he chimed in. "How about when you make an F?" I inquired. "Terrible," he said. I continued, "If you wanted to do something about that F, would you know what to do?" "Yeah," he answered, "study harder." I laughed and said to him, "You know, I hear that all the time. So what does that mean? You'll stick your nose deeper into your book?" The young man couldn't keep the grin off his face. "Well, I guess I could read it." he said.

So what does this little drama have to do with respect? There is almost always the "thought behind the thought." The boy's first reaction was to give the clichè answer that everyone expected to hear. It is the answer that satisfies most parents, and after it is given the conversation usually stops. Curiosity coupled with respect for his ideas leads to the true information, and imparts a sense of significance.

By questioning the boy further I was showing him respect. By asking him questions, I was allowing him to see that he held the real answer. Even the father showed his son respect by bringing him to see me. It would have been very easy for him to scold his son, elicit the stock answer and send him to his room. Instead, he helped the boy find the answer himself.

In so many of our relationships it is easy to react immediately, to cut someone off or disregard his or her views. It's also easy to behave in much more subtle but equally destructive ways. Those behaviors show disrespect, and disrespect destroys relationships.

TONE

In my counseling experience it seemed to me that ninety percent of arguments started with a tone of voice, then each side began looking for issues to support the fight that was already underway. Whenever I say that in a speech to a group, most of the people laugh and nod in agreement.

It seems to happen to me like this: I come home and I'm really tired and my wife says, "Did you have a good day?" In a tone of voice that's less than loving, I reply, "Don't ask." Right away, she gets the feeling that I'm upset. Am I upset at her? Of course not, but she doesn't know that. So she says, "Well, what are you mad about?" "Nothing," I say curtly. "Then why are you talking to me like this?" she says with a hurt tone in her voice.

And there it goes. The fight is underway and it didn't have anything to do with my wife. It occurred because I was tired and arrived with a negative attitude. I expressed no love and I gave her no chance to be loving toward me.

I had a woman tell me, "My husband never comes home right after work!" So I asked her, "What happens when your husband does come home?" "Well, I get on his case," she said without a pause. To which I replied, "I wouldn't come home either. Why would someone come home if they know you are going to yell at them?"

In relationships we should always seek to enhance each other's significance. I hear from many people that they feel their relationships are draining. That is not the true essence of relationships. Loving relationships are energizing.

Helen and I decided many years ago that when we both arrived home after work we would make the first ten minutes "Good Time." We agreed that we would not start the conversation with "Where have you been?" Instead, we would give the other person some breathing room and some time to explain if they were unexpectedly late. We would express appreciation that they were home. It was magic. When we used that time to express our love and appreciation for each other, home became a fun place.

Without exception, this practice puts everything in proper perspective. It takes the edge off the day's tensions. It allows us to see what is truly important. By making a conscious choice to express love, we allow our frustrations to fade and we put our daily "doings" in their proper place. We have the power to set the tone.

These five words I have referred to as CLURT will help you recognize your significance and the significance of others. They are not complex concepts. In fact, they are quite simple. Applying them, however, does require a conscious, mindful effort. We are not trained to stop momentarily, take a deep breath and consider what we can do to be truly helpful. We are trained simply to react, and all of us know that quick reaction usually does not produce the best results. I have found that taking the time to make a conscious effort builds better relationships.

Does God Speak English?

To learn to trust one's feelings over one's observations is indeed a challenge.

P.H.H.

As a young man I first read the Bible out of a sense of obligation. As I grew older I hoped I would find words of truth, words with profound meaning, words that would make me say, "Ohhhhh, now I get it. Now I understand!" I always expected the answers to appear as bold-face type, but that never happened.

I remember sitting down one day with the sole intention of reading the Book of John. I hoped that by reading the whole book I would suddenly gain the understanding that would forever change my life. When I got to the end of the book I had no more understanding than when I started.

When I wasn't reading the Bible searching for the definitive words, I stayed alert for the voice of God to speak directly to me. I was hoping against hope that God would tell me the words that would give my life direction. And, of course, I expected to hear it in English!

I was taught that God had a plan for my life, so I wanted to know what it was. I heard other people talk about how God guided them and sometimes how He actually spoke to them. That's what I wanted! For years I was totally frustrated by what I thought was my inability to hear God's voice.

So I started to re-evaluate my notion of God's voice. I had been expecting words and dialogue, the sound of a voice inside my head or some Scripture to stand out in bold face type.

Then it began to dawn on me. This might happen to some people, but God speaks to me through my imagination. In the Bible it even states, "Whatsoever things you desire, when you pray, believe you receive them and you shall have them." I can have whatever I desire, and then I get to live with that creation for the experience of it – dream, experience, learn, dream…. God simply presents us with the consequences of our choices. God also speaks to us through our feelings. I had learned not to trust my feelings, but now I realized that I had to learn to trust the very thing I had been told I couldn't trust. Listening to God means listening to your true essence – your spirit.

I believe God's energy continually flows through every living thing on earth. The energy carries no judgment – it is pure love. It is then up to me to decide how I want to direct that energy in my life. I can direct it anywhere I decide. When I choose to direct that energy to my highest intention, to that which I believe is my greatest good, I experience well being. When I respond to negativity and direct the energy toward negative thoughts and feelings, I experience dis-ease. Whenever I focus on how to express my joy and creativity, I spark my imagination and respond to my highest good.

When I respond to my highest good, I hear the voice of God in all things. When I wake up in the morning to the sound of the alarm clock or to the songs of birds, I hear the voice of God. I hear the voice of God during cold and still winter nights, and when my apple trees blossom in early spring. I hear it in the laughter of my own voice and in the laughter of others. And I also hear the voice of God when I am stirred by feelings of anger and frustration, and when I listen to people who are in deep emotional pain.

Of course, life continually presents challenges. In difficult times, like the one I had in college, it seemed like God's voice was not present.

I started college immediately after high school, but was unable to continue because of the draft of World War II. Fifteen years later I returned to college and completed my degree when I was 39. I like to say I crammed four years of college into 21 years! When I was 40, I decided to get a master's degree in psychiatric social work. I enrolled at a university in Denver, a school that was quite renowned in the field.

Obviously, I was not a traditional student. What I had learned from my experience in ministry and counseling often proved contrary to what professors were teaching. I thought, naively, that graduate school was a place where a student was supposed to demonstrate an ability to think independently, to ask many questions, and to question many assumptions. Not long after starting the program I began having mixed feelings. I felt the professors treated me and other students in a condescending manner. My questions were ridiculed. What was being taught didn't always seem to fit with what I believed was the nature of social work.

After the second semester I received a letter from the school stating that I was not invited back for the second year of the program. That meant the loss of a scholarship and a monthly stipend. I was devastated. There I was, 40 years old, a family to support, and I'd just been kicked out of school!

I spoke to my advisor and was told that people in the department decided that I had an unconscious desire to fail. She suggested I see a psychiatrist to discuss my "problems." What a shock! Not only had I been asked to leave the school, but the advisor suggested that I might want to get psychiatric help! The psychiatrist refused to take my case. He said I was not there because I thought I had a problem, but just to see if the advisor was right.

As I sorted things out over the next couple of weeks I tried to think about what it was I really wanted. One day I realized that I'd lost my interest in psychiatric social work. What I really wanted was a job as a social worker for a school district. Imagining that job gave me a feeling of great joy, it sparked my imagination. It gave me a feeling much more satisfying than when I thought of returning to graduate school.

A few days later I made an appointment with the local school district to learn about how they used social workers.

I found out they never had one, but were planning to add the position the next month. I applied for the job and became the district's first social worker. That led to a series of opportunities over the next 20 years that were in line with my personal vision for service work. It didn't take long to accept the fact that my dismissal from graduate school had been a blessing.

When I decided to go to graduate school it sparked my imagination. I had a good feeling about it. That was the voice of God. As my feelings began to change about graduate school, even though I didn't fully acknowledge them, the voice of God was speaking to me. When the school asked me to leave, that was God's voice speaking to me in quite a loud tone! And finally, when I imagined the job I really wanted, I acknowledged my highest good and heard the voice of God.

The voice of God is inside each of us, but it does not judge what we perceive as positive or negative. The voice of God only provides what is necessary for us to learn. The voice constantly tells us to accept the intention of the universe and to allow our purpose: to be peaceful, joyful and happy. It is our choice to determine how we will listen and how we will allow God's voice to influence our lives. So, does God speak English?

God speaks to us in every way. Each of us is surrounded by the voice of God; each one of us is the voice of God.

Death or Transition?

The grave is a birth canal.

P.H.H.

Once I stood with a mother at her child's crib. Her seven-month-old boy was dying and she was understandably distraught. She said to me, "Why would God do this to me?" "Well, God didn't," I answered. "Well, who did?" she asked. "Your son did," I replied. She turned quickly to look at me. In a tone of disbelief she demanded, "What do you mean my son did?" I answered slowly. "From our perspective it's hard to see the whole picture. What if his mission in life was to awaken you and your husband to your spiritual dimension. Has he done that?" "Oh yes, he has," the mother answered.

93

The tone of her voice was sincere, even slightly enthusiastic. I continued, "So let's suppose that his job was done. What would you do if your job were finished?" She thought for a moment, then said, "Well, I'd lea...," her voice trailed off momentarily before continuing. "I'd leave." "Maybe your son feels his job is complete. Maybe it is the sense of being incomplete that makes death so difficult," I said.

On almost a daily basis we are faced with trying to make sense of death. Whether it be the death of a loved one, or deaths reported in another part of the world, we are constantly aware that people are dying. And of the prospect of our own death.

Our view of death is learned. Our society's perspective of death is one of tragedy and sorrow. Death is viewed as a loss of control, a plunge into the unknown, a punishment. People learn to fear death and can only view it in terms of tragedy.

The belief that the death of the body is tragic assumes that the essence of life is the physical form. So when our bodies die we are all assigned the same fate – everything ends.

What if we expanded our understanding to recognize that the body is simply a vehicle that expresses spirit for a short time. When the body dies, the spirit changes vehicles. As physical beings we are very attached to our form. That is where most of the emphasis of our lives is placed. What we don't realize is that the essence of life is not the body. The essence of life is spirit. I like the way this is stated in the Bible, "You are in this world, but you are not of this world."

The spirit of each of us is divine perfection, and each of us is an extension and an expression of God. We are not flawed, nothing that happens to us represents a mistake. In perfection, all is well. Why then, should the death of a body be considered a tragedy?

Late in her life my mother started losing her memory. We suspect that she had Alzheimer's Disease, although in those days the condition was known as "senility." During her last five years she had no idea who she was, and she recognized no one. All that we recognized was her body, and her spirit was no longer part of it. When she finally died I did not feel sad, her death was not tragic. What I missed during those last years was her spirit. That is what I loved.

In death, a body changes, but the death of the body is not the end of the spirit. For some, this view treads into difficult territory. Here is a common question I hear: "If we are all perfect spirits, why do people kill each other? Shouldn't we view violent death as tragic?"

Like everyone else, I am stunned by violence and inhumane acts. Murder is an act against a body, an act of the ego based in fear. In spirit there is no fear. The perfect spirit cannot be affected by the acts of another.

After a loved one dies we miss the splendor of their physical presence. Yet, it is spirit that brought forth the beauty, joy and kindness into the body – and the spirit continues.

Many people are afraid to die, or they are afraid of how they will die. They believe death is the end. People say, "What am I going to be remembered for? Who will miss me?"

If I told you that not one person would miss you when you died, would you live your life any differently than you do today? And if I told you that tens of millions of people would mourn and miss you, would you live your life any differently than you do today?

Considering how we will be remembered is strictly an act of the ego. The ego searches outside for answers and approval. Approval from the outside is meaningless to the true self, to the spirit.

About ten years ago a doctor who had practiced at our local hospital died. He was very well known in the community and some people got together and built a memorial rose garden on the hospital grounds. There is a small plaque there with his name on it.

Every day fewer and fewer people remember him, but that doesn't diminish his accomplishments on earth, nor does it mean he didn't spread enough love while he lived in his physical form. It certainly doesn't mean his spirit is dead.

Many times over the years I have been present at the moment when people have made their transitions. Some are paralyzed by fear until their last breath. They seem to be the ones who have lived tentatively, unsure or unwilling to express their joy or their love, or have lived with sadness, regret and fear.

I also have been with dying people who have embraced life, laughed hard, cried hard, and loved fully. It is not unusual for their homes or hospital rooms to be filled with friends laughing and talking. At those gatherings there is little sense of tragedy because it is clear that the person who is dying is participating fully in the process. The body is the temporary physical expression of a spirit that cannot die.

I lead many memorial services each year. The first thing I do is meet with the family and ask them to describe the person. Almost without exception, those meetings become sessions full of laughter and tears. What is remembered, usually, are not the accomplishments, but the spirit of the person. Family members tell wonderful stories of how the person loved and laughed. At the same time they are free to tell stories about unpleasant memories and the difficult times, thus allowing them to express the full spectrum of their connections and their emotions.

Using those stories I am able to lead a service that truly celebrates the spirit, and allows people to remember and be thankful for all the times they had together. A memorial service is a time for us to cry and to laugh. It is a time to give attention to the total range of emotions that put us in touch with our spirits, and with the spirit that has left the physical form.

By acknowledging spirit, you are in touch with all that is. When you accept life as being much more than a physical experience, death can be viewed as transformation, not tragedy.

At memorial services I always tell this story. Many years ago I worked with kids in Sunday school and we always talked about the wonders of nature. One day a boy brought in a caterpillar. We put it in a cup and I set it on my desk. A couple of days later I looked into the cup and the caterpillar was gone. Figuring that it had crawled away, I forgot about it. A week later I walked into my office and saw a chrysalis, a fuzzy cocoon, hanging from the corner of my desk. I realized that the caterpillar was in the process of metamorphosis. Again, I forgot about the chrysalis until a couple of days later when I opened the window. I stood there for a moment and a small yellow butterfly suddenly appeared and flew out the window. Initially I was puzzled, wondering how a butterfly got into the office. Then I remembered the chrysalis, walked to it, and saw it hanging there empty.

For spirit, the transition of death is like a caterpillar during metamorphosis. We fear death because it represents an end. For spirit, the death of the body is simply a transformation.

What happens when you are walking on a hiking trail? As you look ahead to a bend in the path, you don't stop because you can't see everything that's ahead. You approach the unknown with wonder, excitement and curiosity.

It is in the same way that we can choose to view death. Not as an ending, but as another step in our spiritual experience. If the essence of our being is spirit, and spirit is eternal and not bound by time and space, then doesn't it follow that death has only to do with the car, not the driver?

Redefining Perfection

Perfection is being in process, not completion.
P.H.H.

Several years ago I was asked to talk to a 14-year-old young lady who was seven months pregnant. According to the person making the referral, this young lady was not demonstrating much responsibility toward her unborn child. When I talked to her, she spoke in excessively vulgar language and showed very little respect for her mother or for those who were trying to assist her. She also had an amazing capacity to bring out the worst in me.

She gave birth to a baby girl. After about three months, the baby was placed in a foster home due to inadequate care. After many attempts to reach a reasonable level of communication with her, I finally said, "No more!" "No more what?" she asked. "I refuse to believe that your behavior tells me who you are. I believe that there is a perfect girl in there somewhere. From now on I will only speak to that perfect girl that I know is buried in there somewhere." "Perfect like Hell" was her only response.

Just a few days later she was detained by the police and sent to a juvenile holding facility where she remained for over a month. When she returned home, she asked for an appointment. Her first words to me when we were in my office were, "Did you say 'there's a perfect girl in here'?" she said pointing to herself. "Yes," I said. "I've decided to let her out," she declared.

From that point on, there were no more missed appointments, no more profanity, only questions as to why she behaved the way she did. She stopped fighting for custody of her child because she knew she was not in a position to provide for the child's welfare.

It would appear that when we get in touch with the perfection which lies within, no matter how deeply buried, we then make decisions more compatible with what is good for all concerned.

A verse in the book of Genesis says that we are created "in the image and likeness of God." In the New Testament it is said that "God hath put His spirit within us." Consider the beauty of that! When we think of God, we think of a pure and beautiful spirit. We believe that God is the very essence of perfection. So if we are created in the image and likeness of God, it is apparent that we too have that place within us that expresses the perfection of God. Each of us has a pure and perfect spirit within.

Of course, such an idea is rejected by most. We hear quite often that "no one is perfect." We have been told that only God is perfect, and that the best we can ever do is strive for perfection. What if we think of perfection as movement in the direction of a goal rather than a plateau of achievement?

Imagine yourself standing directly on top of the North Pole. If you choose to move, you can travel in just one direction – south. It doesn't matter where you are going from there, any step you take will be in the right direction. All of us talk about the direction of our lives. We say, "I'm headed in the wrong direction," or "I want to get my life going in a different direction." So imagine for a moment that the North Pole is your spiritual base. It is that perfect position where you hold your sense of self and where your inner spirit is peaceful. Things then make sense and directions are clear.

If you are operating from your spiritual base, in what direction will your life go? It can only go one way. It can only go in the direction you intend for it to go. It can only go in the right direction, which is the direction of your joy and contentment. There are no wrong directions! There can be no wrong directions! From the base of the perfect spirit it is easy to step into life with great enthusiasm.

When I tell people this they ask me, "How do I know when I am standing on my North Pole?" It is easy to start analyzing and looking at things like your job, your relationships and your fears. Those are the typical starting points for most people when they begin to analyze their lives. The problem is, most of those things we did not create from our

North Pole. We start analyzing the "doing" of our lives instead of the "being."

To find your spiritual North Pole, sit quietly and think of the space where you feel most at home, the place where you feel warm, comfortable and safe. The place where it's easy to think clearly, where your spirit is calm. If you allow it, that is a place of great beauty that comes from within.

Think for a moment of a geode. From the outside, the geode looks like a plain old rock. But inside it is dazzling and beautiful. The inside, not the outside, is the true essence of the geode.

The same is true for you. You are not your body, your job or your house. It is the beauty that you hold inside that expresses your true nature. Deep inside, deep at home, you hold your truth. In that place you express your joy.

When you allow yourself to feel that peace, when you allow yourself to feel completely at home, you are at your spiritual North Pole. It is from that basis that you can most effectively make your choices in life. It is easy to know that you are making decisions based on your joy.

When all of your decisions are based on your joy it is impossible to make a wrong decision. You know your spiritual home. It is impossible to go in the wrong direction.

It is possible to perpetually stand at your spiritual North Pole. In all things you do it is possible to proceed in only one direction, the direction of your joy, excitement and inspiration.

When our children were in their teens, if you had asked how they were doing, I would have said, "They are perfect teenagers." Would that mean they didn't make the typical mistakes teenagers make? Or would it mean that they were where one would expect them to be at that age on their path to maturity?

You may have heard it said that corn is supposed to be knee high by the fourth of July. If we walked out into a cornfield on July 4th and the corn reached our knees even without ears and tassels, we would say, "perfect."

These experiences have led me to ask: Is it presumptuous to think of ourselves as less than what God created us to be? To deny that we are less than perfect is to deny that we are created "in the image and likeness of God."

What if we looked at it this way. I am as God created me. Now I am learning how to bring my behavior into alignment with my true essence.

Within each of us lives the pure and perfect essence, the true nature of our being. It doesn't matter where you're from, or your religious or cultural training. Every person is the embodiment of the perfect spirit. We have the choice to either awaken to that spirit or to keep it buried.

Several passages from the Bible refer to this shift in perspective; "Be ye perfect even as your Father in heaven is perfect," and, "For in Him we live and move and have our being.... For we are also His offspring."

Perfection has acquired a meaning that signifies a final plateau of achievement, but for the universe, for our spirit, there is no plateau. The real meaning of perfection is to continually be growing in our expression of love. I think of perfection as a direction, rather than as an achievement. There can be no plateau for the expression of love!

I believe that what we give our attention to expands. If we continually give attention to our imperfection, that thought begins to loom so large that we eventually forget the perfection that lies within. If we believe in a God who judges and punishes imperfection, then it becomes almost impossible to recognize our spirit, which is perfect.

As a dear friend of ours points out, there are always two aspects to any subject: its presence or its absence. There are times when we forget and do not express our true essence. When we are distressed or angry or depressed, then we express our false identity – that which we are not. The universe doesn't respond to how things should be. It responds perfectly to the thoughts we hold.

Now what if instead of wallowing in fear, anger or guilt, you choose to bask in joy. To recognize that you are whole in your being, that there is nothing to fix, nothing to fear, and that all your experiences are part of the pure, positive flow of the universe? You begin to identify who you are by listening to your perfect spirit. You see a flow of love everywhere you look. You attract patience and understanding. Peace fills your heart and you recognize the same pure perfection in everyone, no matter how they are behaving.

The joy and the love vibrate. The pendulums on the clocks swing together. That is synchronicity. When you recognize your perfection and the perfection of others, you are in harmony and effortlessly find your own truth. Gone are the "should haves" and the "ought tos." Your life becomes a *journey to happiness.*

The spirit of your being stands in that moment. You are in harmony with the universe. When you choose your perfection, you cause it to expand. You are destined to choose perfection as your course. Accept your inner voice and the leading of the heart as the guide of your true spirit.

Even in difficult situations, choose to follow the course of joy. Allow the spirit that is within you to achieve expression; choose the perfection that is within. You know it is the truth. Now live it!

ABOUT PAUL HOLDEMAN

My journey started more than 70 years ago. I grew up in a home where the church was the focus of family activities. The literal interpretation of the Bible was my family's guide for personal responsibility. It was also an accurate predictor of world events.

My earliest memories begin soon after my family had suffered the devastation of repeated flooding of our farm in Missouri. My father decided that he would rather "blow out than drown out," so we moved to western Kansas. We were just recovering from the flood losses when the depression and the drought of the 1930s again devastated the farming business. Our best wheat crop sold at a substantial loss. For three years in a row, western Kansas received less than half the average rainfall. As the grass and grain crops dried up we sold all of our cow herd for less than our investment. Then my parents lost all of their cash when the local bank failed.

Even though I was just seven-years-old and the youngest of seven kids, I was keenly aware of the profound loss my parents were experiencing. And our family wasn't alone. Neighbors, friends, and many other people across the country lost everything of material value.

When we viewed all of this from the perspective of literal biblical prophecy, we believed we were living in the "last days," the times of "trouble and tribulation." Sermons at our church offered no hope for this world. We believed, in accordance with our interpretation of the Bible, that the anti-Christ would deceive almost everyone and make the world obedient to Satan. Only the true believers would be saved.

Fortunately, during those difficult days, my parents began to reconsider their beliefs about biblical prophesy, formal education and politics. Times were tough, but tribulation or not, we had work to do. Our home was a happy one and I knew I was loved, even though displays of affection were rare.

As a second grader, I watched my parents and older siblings start changing their thinking about the world. They began to view what had previously appeared to be negative events with a more discerning eye. They began to recognize that those events also presented opportunities beyond anything they'd known before. Our house became a place of intellectual adventure as each member of the family came home every day with new insights on life, spirit and religion. I also started to hear hopeful tales from the world beyond the farm.

What I didn't realize at the time was that I was being shown a profoundly new way to look at the world. We redefined our ideas about God, faith, spirit and church...and about ourselves.

My family started choosing new ideas that flew in the face of our conservative religious training. My parents held the courage to live their own truth.

The church my family belonged to had many branches with varying degrees of conservative theology. When I was very young we belonged to a branch that opposed education beyond the minimum legal limit. My parents disagreed with that idea and resigned to join another branch that supported higher education. Members of the old branch treated my parents and older siblings as outcasts. But our new affiliation provided a stimulating social and intellectual environment for my family. All of us were now encouraged to get as much education as possible. Our mother reminded us, however, that formal education "either educates a wise person or a fool."

In a closely-knit agricultural community my parents action required great courage. By making the break, they pursued their truth and provided their children with a profound example of personal integrity. They risked everything to follow their principles – they knew they had no other choice.

Unfortunately, my father was not able to enjoy the results of his decision. At the very height of his passion to see his children educated far beyond his own achievement, he developed a brain tumor that slowly killed him. Yet, at the moment he died we shared an experience that forever shaped my view of life, death and spirit.

I was 15 years old; standing at the foot of his bed. For two weeks he had been motionless. His mouth hung open, his unseeing-eyes stared blankly. We had spent most of our lives with a robust and vigorous man who loved the work of the farm, so it was difficult for us to see him in that condition. Suddenly, his eyes widened and a smile spread across his face. His head rolled to one side and he gazed with what appeared to be wonderment up into a corner of the room. Within a few minutes his breathing stopped.

Whatever my father saw, I knew that it was good. He was looking beyond his physical boundaries. It was not until many years later, however, that I would begin to grasp the significance of what my father had experienced. That the spiritual gives us much more than we can experience in these bodies.

I didn't know it then, but that was the beginning of an ongoing personal journey of spiritual discovery. Through the years I have employed an intentional effort to question, and if necessary, change my view of the world. At every step I have been presented with opportunities to view my life and the world in one of two ways – with love or with fear.

In fear I manifested many problems and chose to make my life a struggle. When I embraced love – of myself and of the world – things changed dramatically. Joy replaced judgment and a peaceful attitude helped remove doubt and despair.

Just 17 months after my father died, Pearl Harbor was bombed and war engulfed the world. We were avowed pacifists, holding firmly to the belief that "they that take the sword shall perish by the sword." At a young age I found that my beliefs contradicted those of most people in the country. Frequently, this is what my brothers and I heard: "Forget your Bible, we are in a war."

When I was drafted, I refused to join the military, but accepted alternative service as a firefighter in Glacier National Park. At times I felt uneasy about how I was serving my country, so during those quiet days in Montana, I began an internal quest to examine the beliefs of the church and of my values. The result was that I became firmly convinced that I wanted to be a person of peace in the world and that I could not be part of the process of hate.

My quest, however, presented me with an unexpected discovery. I learned that although I refused to participate in war, it was not necessary for me to judge those who did. With this discovery I was at liberty to explore a much broader world, and I learned to cast off the fear of new ideas. By choosing to look through the eyes of love, I began to see the world as a much different place. I lost my reluctance to express my point of view, even when I knew I would be criticized.

It was during this time in my life that I met Helen, who three years later became my wife. She was a free soul who found it unnecessary to make a display of her independent thoughts and ways – she just lived them. At first I thought that she didn't think things through as well as I did. But in time I learned the truth of the adage: "You teach best that which you most need to learn." Helen did not need to articulate her freedom, but I did because I needed to learn that I had it.

We were both reared in the same denomination and our interests were similar. We were taught that the world did not owe us anything, but that we did owe the world our service. For that lesson we have been profoundly grateful. Helen found that nursing offered her the best opportunity to give that service. I was much slower in coming to clarity.

Work within the church appealed to me, and I was especially attracted to the worldwide service mission of our church. The church, however, was a paradox for me. Although it gave me opportunities, it also was a source of some emotional pain and confusion. Now I understand that those experiences provided perfect lessons that helped guide my life's journey.

Helen and I were married in 1948 and eventually we raised four children. During the first year of marriage I said to Helen, "Let's not stay together because we are married."

"What do you mean?" she asked.

"Let's stay together because we want to," I answered.

Without hesitation, she agreed. Those words became our guiding principle in those early years. During stressful times we continually made a conscious choice to stay together.

Over the years we felt free to challenge traditional religious views and to create our own spiritual path, but we always held the belief that we should be of service to the world. The belief in service provided a guide for my spiritual search and my life's work as a student, teacher, family counselor, probation counselor, and spiritual counselor for several churches (the terms "minister" and "reverend" are uncomfortable for me).

While in the service of a church in Texas I raised questions about traditional beliefs and customs. My ideas and my questions struck a positive chord with some of the congregation members, but others were disturbed and they brought my dissenting opinions to the attention of regional leaders. In less than two years I accepted an invitation from another denomination in the same town to work in its youth program and to assist the pastor.

Later, I worked as an assistant pastor and in youth programs for another church in Colorado where I was asked to pursue a seminary degree. I declined. That opened the path for my career as a social worker for a school, and later as a probation counselor for juveniles.

In 1987 I was teaching a class for people who had been arrested for driving under the influence. A man in the class liked my approach and invited me to speak one Sunday at the church he attended in Fort Collins, Colorado.

Eventually, the board asked me to stay. While the fit was extraordinary, I was wary of becoming "the minister." Helen and I had no interest in another traditional church structure. So, when the church board asked me to stay, we set down four conditions:

1. I would never attempt to inspire guilt regarding attendance. I would never say to anyone, "We missed you." I would only say, "We're glad to see you."

2. I would never inspire guilt about financial contributions. We should not give to support a church, but to create flow for ourselves.

3. I made no promises that next Sunday's lesson would sound anything like the past Sunday's lesson. I explained that I am a growing and changing person and that the lessons would reflect that.

4. I would make no attempt to drum up energy for something for which no energy exists. In every organization projects are started, usually because someone in a "leadership position" believes they should be. I believe a pro-

ject should continue only if people believe it should be done and are willing to expend the effort and attract others. A project should not proceed just because "the leadership" says so. The energy that expresses spirit will be supported not because of our efforts, but because it provides a joyful connection.

The board agreed. In this church we have no "membership," and people contribute what we need to grow. Many individuals attempt to start projects or programs, some of them succeed, some of them do not. Either way, the outcome is as it should be. We have a lot of fun. We laugh. In fact, we believe the more laughter the better. As one man says, "I like to come here on Sunday because then I don't have to go to church."

Helen and I find our situation exhilarating. It took 40 years for us to arrive in a place where we feel we are aligned with spirit. And we could not have arrived here without all the steps we've taken. We did not always trust our *journey to happiness;* but, in hindsight, it unfolded perfectly!

Helen and I have a favorite verse in Mark, the eleventh chapter – "Whatsoever things ye desire when you pray, believe you receive them and you shall have them." It is my belief that our thoughts are our prayers and all of us are constantly praying. Sometimes the prayers are fearful, angry and full of judgment. Other times they are full of joy and love. Whichever gets our attention eventually gets us. I do know this for certain: All of us are entitled to fulfill our deepest desires; everyone deserves to be surrounded by love and filled with joy...*Homemade Joy!*